Cañon City
Colorado

THIS CONVENIENT MAP WILL GUIDE YOU TO ALL POINTS OF INTEREST IN THE ROYAL GORGE REGION

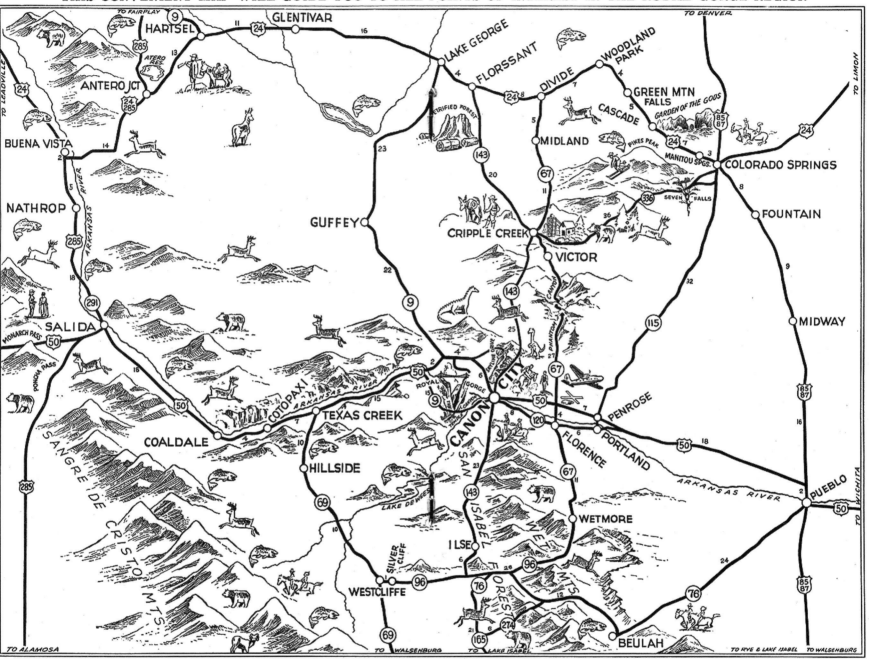

Crossing the Arkansas River, C. 1890.

Cañon City Colorado

Every Picture Tells A Story

By
Larry Thomas Ward

Nicholas Lawrence Books

Los Angeles ☆ Cañon City, Colorado

Dedicated To

Additional copies of this book can be obtained by calling 1-800-574-7438.

Library of Congress Control Number: 2005920405

ISBN 0-9729466-4-0

Printed in the United States of America

Second Edition

CONTENTS

Cañon City
Colorado

—•••—

In The Beginning...
A Brief History

PROSPECTORS.

Local History Center, Cañon City

In The Beginning...
A Brief History

The town was meant to be nothing more than a way station for miners and prospectors heading to the gold fields of South Park. When William Kroenig and his partners first established Cañon City in October of 1859, they could not have imagined what the future held for this city along the Arkansas.

The area around Cañon City, and especially along the Arkansas River near Soda Point, had long been a favorite campground for Native Americans. Members of both the Ute and Cheyenne tribes would drink from the Iron Springs and bathe in the bubbling water of the nearby hot springs. An occasional prospector or trapper would quietly wander through the valley on a quest for an uncomplicated life, but few stopped to take notice of its ancient beauty, or mused about what could be. Other wanderers included adventurers such as Zebulon Pike during the winter of 1806, and explorer John C. Fremont in the 1840s, from whom Fremont County derives its name.

On March 13, 1860, the Cañon City Claim Club, headed by William Kroenig, was organized to promote the newly formed town as a viable, prosperous, and permanent settlement. When gold was found in California Gulch, prospectors paraded through Cañon City in droves. Lively merchants were there to greet them, selling everything from fresh eggs to blankets. A sawmill was soon delivered from Minnesota, and a shingle mill was built along Sand

Local History Center, Cañon City

John C. Fremont, 1890.

Creek. To handle the sudden influx of both people and merchandise, large sheds were hastily constructed to store the tons of flour and vegetables to be readied for shipment by horse drawn freighters to the mining camps many miles away. And six months later, in September of 1860, H. S. Millet became the editor of the *Cañon City Times*, the town's first newspaper. Homes were being built at an alarming rate, and when winter came hundreds more arrived from the surrounding mines, filling the town as never before. As Rosemae Wells Campbell describes in her excellent *From Trappers to Tourists*, "That winter Cañon City was a wide-open, wild town. Every department of pleasure ran at capacity." Saloons became numerous and those who frequented them also found pleasure in ways that did not involve drinking or gambling. General courtesy and basic manners were lax or non-existent, midnight brawls were commonplace, and gunfights occurred on a regular basis. Men were shot over petty grievances; still others, for even less, such as the case of Charles Dodge who "shot and killed three men who irked him." Horse stealing resulted in similar frontier justice – death by hanging.

When the spring of 1861 arrived, the rowdy miners, prospectors and cowboys headed back to the mines, to the collective relief of the remaining townsfolk. But several dozen men vowed not to waste another year seeking lost treasure, and instead took up farming.

One man who did not leave was Anson P. Rudd. He had arrived the prior August with his new bride, Harriet – after an eighteen year courtship. Intending to stay only through the winter, Harriet convinced Anson to make Cañon City their home; and so they did, building a log cabin on the northeast corner of Fourth and Main Streets. Years later, the cabin was displaced for the McClure House, and moved to a spot directly behind the Cañon City Municipal Museum, where it can be visited today. Known for his elaborate poetry, and because he was the town's blacksmith, Rudd was immediately dubbed the "Blacksmith Poet." He would soon also take the informal name of Anson, "Sr.", as his son of the same first name – Anson Spencer – would be born. For years it was circulated and widely believed that Anson Spencer Rudd was the first white child born in Cañon City to survive infancy, but decades later others came forward with differing opinions strongly suggesting the contrary. The matter is still unresolved.

The summer of 1861 was an unprofitable one for most prospectors, as easy gold dust had eluded them. Some left the territory, while still others also tried farming with little success. Just when they were preparing for another long winter, recruiting officers from the Union Army came calling. The army was anticipating a war between the states, and in just a matter of a few days, they effectively rounded up what few able-bodied men were left in the town. The population was down to

Local History Center, Cañon City

Anson P. Rudd and Anson S. Rudd, 1867.

Local History Center, Cañon City

Harriet Rudd, 1849.

Local History Center, Cañon City

Anson Rudd's 1860 log cabin.

a mere dozen, with Rudd later joking that after excluding invalids and the deranged, he was the only real man left in town.

Over the next three years, times were hard. Crops failed and few of the mines remained open. At one point, in 1864, Rudd became sheriff, then inspector of distilled spirits and oil for the federal government. He later became a county commissioner, then the postmaster of Cañon City. His postmaster's job was one that held a dubious distinction, since the city had no mail – coming or going.

The outlook for the town's survival looked bleak, and all was thought lost – until the wagon train arrived.

They were a group of twenty-two families from Missouri that had traveled almost three months before arriving in Cañon City. The trail from the Midwest was long, hot and dusty, often filled with danger and violence from bandits and outlaws. The Arkansas River was as much a welcome sight to these families as the families were to Rudd. These were the families that would resurrect the town, and their names are still familiar to us today. They were the Macons, the Harrisons, and the McClures.

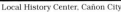
Local History Center, Cañon City

Main Street, C. 1865.

The resurrectionists were of the Baptist faith and soon established a congregation, while the members of the already established Methodist Episcopal Church found space at a building at 228 Main Street. By 1867, the Cumberland Presbyterian Church had been built on the corner of Macon and Fifth Streets, where the Cañon City Public Library now rests. The town could now count forty families as permanent residents, and with the post office reopening in the basement of the Fremont House (where the Deputy Warden's house is now located,) everyone felt and believed that the hard times were over.

At the conclusion of the Civil War, many more families arrived back to the "Gate City to the Mountains," including George Rockafellow and his son, Captain Benjamin (B. F.) Rockafellow. By 1869, both the South Cañon Ditch and the Garden Park Ditch were irrigating the farm lands. Henry Harrison had planted a large orchard, and the Rockafellows were platting an area southeast of town that they named Lincoln Park, in honor of Abraham Lincoln. Cañon City's first public school – a large room in Bates Hall – held its first classes with teacher Nellie Virden Morford.

Local History Center, Cañon City

Settlers arriving in Cañon City, C. 1870.

Local History Center, Cañon City

Main Street, C. 1870.

In a promotional tract first published by the town's founding fathers – "Published By Authority of the Citizens of Fremont County" – and written by A. E. Mathews in 1870, a formal effort was thus underway to begin attracting new settlers to Cañon City to become fruit farmers. In showcasing the town he writes that Cañon City had "one drug store, one boot and shoe store, one harness and saddlers shop, two blacksmiths' shops, one excellent flouring mill, two hotels, one butcher's shop, and one feed stable; and here, too, is located the Territorial Penitentiary, which is a fine structure, costing over thirty-six thousand dollars."

The promotion proved to be a simple testing of the waters for county leaders, as the real push to create an agrarian society would not take shape until the 1880s. Until that time, the city was busy with other matters, such as promoting the health advantages of the revered Soda and Iron Springs, and creating the "Old Settlers Reunion," a precursor to the Fruit Day celebrations.

Cañon City incorporated in 1872, with George Rockafellow becoming its first mayor. In the following year, the long-anticipated Denver & Rio Grande Railroad (D&RG) finally showed signs of coming to Cañon City. What resulted is the now infamous Royal Gorge War between the D&RG and the Santa Fe Railroad, with the latter eventually winning the honor of building the track through the Royal Gorge, but later returning the route to D&RG. Doris Osterwald's *Rails Thru the Gorge* offers an interesting and valuable history of this time, with great insight and an obvious love for railroad lore.

The year of 1874 brought two banks to Cañon City, James Clelland's Cañon City Bank, and twenty-four year old Fred Raynold's Fremont County Bank. Raynolds headquartered his local financial empire in William McClure's newly-opened hotel, the McClure House at Fourth and Main Streets, only later to build his own bank building.

The Cañon City Arbor and Floricultural Society was formed to "encourage planting of fruit and shade trees, flowers, grasses, and ornamental or fruit bearing shrubs." The push was on to turn the barren city landscape into a garden city, and the group did just that, planting more than one thousand shade trees, most along Main Street. The great cottonwoods grew straight and tall, and as irony

Early photograph of a heavily treed Macon Avenue, 1880.

would have it, in time, almost all were later cut down as commercial development increased throughout town.

Benjamin Rockafellow was elected mayor in 1876, the year of this young country's centennial. To celebrate, there were parades, a balloon ascension, and speeches by Anson Rudd, Fred Raynolds and Thomas Macon. County officials talked of opening its first county poorhouse for the disadvantaged, along with its first county jail at 104 Greenwood Avenue. In the same year, brick baron William Catlin offered ten acres of land to the city for the creation of the Greenwood Cemetery, with specific sections set aside for various populations, such as plots for the poor, inmates from prison, unclaimed remains of prisoners, GAR and confederate veterans, and a host of Catlins.

Ormel W. Lucas, a teacher at Garden Park, found the first of many dinosaur bones along a seven mile stretch of hills at Fourmile Creek now known as Museum Range. While few locals were genuinely interested in such matters, with one newspaper editor calling the range the "bone yard," the

Local History Center, Cañon City

Stagecoach to Westcliffe, C. 1880.

subsequent finds resulted in some of paleontology's most important discoveries. The Dinosaur Depot on Royal Gorge Boulevard continues the work of these early scientists.

By 1878, Cañon City boasted a population of about five hundred residents. Daily stagecoach lines began hauling passengers to Westcliffe and back (seven hours each way) for about two dollars roundtrip. Anson Rudd, Henry Harrison, Warren Fowler and several others created the Cañon City Hydraulic & Irrigation Ditch Company. The company was formed to maintain the Cañon City Fourmile Ditch that served to irrigate Harrison's two-thousand acres of orchards. Other wealthy citizens also formed the Cañon City Water Company for similar purposes.

After years of delays, the first excursion train through the Royal Gorge carried two hundred passengers from Cañon City to Parkdale on May 7, 1879. The improbable Hanging Bridge had just been completed at the deepest and most narrow stretch of the gorge. For the first time, the bridge finally allowed trains to traverse along and above the edge of the Arkansas River.

The following year of 1880 brought the construction of the town's first public school building, a handsome three-story structure made from bricks manufactured at the prison. Later named Washington School, each room had its own coal stove. The school would be in use for seventy years before being razed in 1957.

It was in the same year that the county built its first courthouse in Cañon City, an impressively large red stone structure located at First Street and Macon Avenue.

The Colorado Collegiate and Military Institute was also organized in 1880, and served primarily as a military school for high school students. It was the first such school in Cañon City, and it set the standard for all high school military training yet to come. When the school finally closed less than five years later, the building became the new home for Mount Saint Scholastica Academy.

Dall DeWeese, a wealthy cattleman and fruit farmer from Glenwood Springs, arrived in Cañon City around 1884. Not coincidentally, it was at the same time that the final push to have the Cañon City area designated as a farming region took place. It was generally promoted that with the state of mining in a slight decline, with no other commerce on the horizon, it was the only logical and viable course of action for citizens to follow. And follow they did.

DeWeese immediately purchased over one-thousand acres in South Cañon and began an ingenious plan to irrigate the entire valley through a mighty array of various ditches and reservoirs. In cooperation with several other wealthy Cañon City citizens – Fred Raynolds, Henry Harrison, and William McClure, the power brokers of the era – they embarked on what essentially proved to be a twenty year plan to turn the entire region into fruit farms and orchards – and they succeeded.

Local History Center, Cañon City

Henry Harrison (far right) standing on the picker
platform at his apple orchard, C. 1911.

Cañon City Fruit Farm Workers, C. 1890.

In her paper, "Establishing An Irrigation-Based Society," LaDonna L. Gunn argues, convincingly, that because this group of "elite capitalists" controlled the water – vital to a town's existence – they ultimately also thought they could control who lived there. By irrigating the land, planting fruit trees and small orchards, and then subdividing the area into forty and fifty acre plots, they could dictate the migration of a certain class of people, or create an entire society comprised of a choice selection of people. In this case, the group priced their plots high enough that they excluded all but the wealthy buyer. And so it was that in due course, the Cañon City area, almost overnight in agricultural terms, was transformed into one of the most agriculturally productive centers in the West. However, what DeWeese and the others had not considered was that by recruiting the "better class," as they stated, they also inadvertently created an under-class, the labor class. Who else to actually work the fields?

The agricultural labor class in Cañon City in the 1890s, and well into the 1930s, consisted primarily of poor, unemployed and underemployed farm laborers. While a large percentage of these workers were male, an equal number were female – and children. It was hard work, and quite often entire families would be pressed into service during the fall apple harvest season. In fact, the harvest was such an important part of the county's economy that education was frequently sacrificed in the name of production. Several school districts would close for months on end while children worked alongside their mothers or fathers. These jobs provided badly needed income for struggling families, but at laborer wages. To be sure, it was honest and honorable work, and the mild climate eased the physical hardship often associated with farming, yet few managed to break the social barrier that bound them to these farms.

Toward the end of the nineteenth century, there came two additional changes in the community that helped shape its future: a free library, and Guy Hardy's acquisition of the *Cañon City Record*.

Cañon City's wealthiest and most influential ladies came to a consensus that the city was badly in need of a free lending library. So through a series of fund raising methods, and with a collective

Sitting in his carriage is B.F. Rockafellow, 1892
at the corner of Seventh and Main Streets.

resolve that was unshakeable, the first such facility was developed in an older building on Main Street. In time, a new and carefully designed Carnegie Library was later constructed on Macon Avenue, where it remains today.

Guy Hardy was twenty-three years old when he started as a reporter for the *Cañon City Record*. But by 1895, he had talked the publisher into selling him the newspaper. Thus began a long and rich history of several members of the Hardy family becoming involved in the newspaper business during the life of several generations. At first a weekly paper, it became a daily in 1906, and remains Cañon City's dominant newspaper today.

Guy Hardy later became Congressman Hardy in the Territorial Legislature, and it was he who persuaded the federal government to convey to Cañon City the area known as the Royal Gorge.

Local History Center, Cañon City

Guy Hardy, C. 1905.

Just after 1900, inmate labor from the Territorial Prison was utilized to build Skyline Drive and Priest Canyon Road, just as they had built Tunnel Drive. The first automobile in town, a 1901 Oldsmobile, was owned by Dr. Frank Bartlett, with dentist G. H. Kellenberger owning the second, also an Olds. By 1905, eight such vehicles were breezing through the city, traumatizing both large horses and small children.

Between 1900 and 1930: Dr. Levi B. Ward established Ward Hospital on Macon Avenue with eighteen physicians treating tuberculosis patients. Benjamin Rockafellow sold his Fruitmere orchards to a group of Benedictine monks from Pennsylvania. They, in turn, used part of the land to build the Holy Cross Abbey. Company C of the Colorado National Guard in Cañon City actively sought Pancho Villa at the Mexican border in 1916. The film industry came to the city in 1910 and Cañon City

Local History Center, Cañon City

Dr. G. H. Kellenberger driving Cañon City's
second automobile, a 1901 Oldsmobile.

suddenly – and only briefly – became the filmmaking capital of the West, hosting legendary cowboy star Tom Mix, along with many others. The KKK had an obvious and unfortunate presence in the city in the 1920s, but were gone by the 1930s. And in 1929, the Suspension Bridge spanning the Royal Gorge was completed. It remains Cañon City's most visited tourist attraction.

By the mid-1930s, the Benedictine Sisters of South Dakota bought the vacant YMCA building at Fifth Street and Macon Avenue. Having also purchased the former Holmes

Ward Collection

Apple Orchard with heaters, 1909.

Hospital at Fifth Street and Greenwood Avenue, they remodeled the YMCA building into a fifty-bed hospital. They named it the St. Thomas More Hospital. This building faithfully served the Cañon City and surrounding communities until the 1960s when the new hospital on Phay Avenue was constructed.

Dall DeWeese died in 1928 at the age of seventy-one years, but before doing so, he offered to give to the city his vast collection of wild animal trophies gathered over a period of forty years. His only condition was that the town provide an appropriate setting with which to display his lifeless menagerie. The city council allocated sixty thousand dollars for the construction of a new municipal building, of which the second floor would be used to exhibit DeWeese's rare collection. Now called the Municipal Museum, the DeWeese collection and other holdings continue to attract many visitors to this day.

Not long after the death of Dall DeWeese, the agriculture industry in Cañon City was on the wane. From 1880 to 1930, more than thirty-thousand acres in the area had been irrigated, yet only ten-thousand acres had actually been utilized for that purpose. In addition to DeWeese, the Rockafellows,

Ward Collection

The Municipal Building, 1938.

ONE DAYS SPORT.

A RECORD MOOSEHEAD
OF THE WORLD 69 INCH SPREAD
KILLED IN ALASKA
BY DALL DE WEESE CANON CITY COLO.
1897.
COPYRIGHT

Dall DeWeese, 1899.

Henry Harrison, Anson Rudd, Fred Raynolds, and William McClure – all were gone, and the drive to maintain Cañon City as an agricultural paradise seemed to die with them. By the end of World War II, the local men and women who had worked the fields – and the generation to follow – sought other ways to make a living. Fruit prices had dropped and manufacturing plants in Pueblo began offering better wages. In time, the orchards made way for housing developments, and the always-active canning factories dwindled until there were none. The combination of these events spelled an abrupt end to mass commercial fruit farming in Cañon City.

Local History Center, Cañon City

Bird's Eye View of Cañon City, 1905.

The Soda and Mineral Iron Springs
U.S. Highway 50

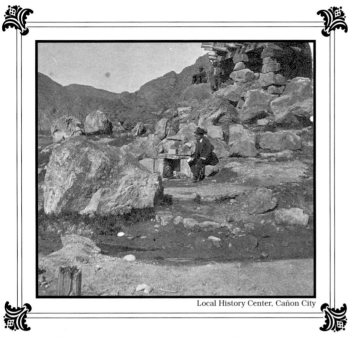

Local History Center, Cañon City

Union soldier resting at the mouth
of the Soda Springs, 1864.

On a small patch of land at the southern point of the hogbacks lay an area long known to Cañon City residents as Soda Point. It was at this spot that for more than eighty years couples would stop after a long walk to refresh themselves with the water from the Soda Springs. It was here that romances often blossomed, and it was here that families would come for the freshly-made lemonade or buy ice cream from the town's first vendor of frozen delicacies.

Long before the arrival of Cañon City's permanent residents, the Utes and other Native American tribes found the Soda Springs to be rich in minerals. They used this water not to quench thirst, but for medicinal purposes. The springs were revered as a natural healer of physical and spiritual ills.

Zebulon Pike camped nearby in 1806, and he mentioned the unusual quality of the water in his written reports. His small party found the water to be rejuvenating and pure.

It was not until about 1864 that a formal effort was made to capture the water for public use by fashioning small stone basins around the springs. There were actually two springs, one that dispensed water heavy with iron and unpleasant in taste, and the other known as Soda Springs; its water had a cold, clean and refreshing taste. This was the water that residents would walk miles to drink – and come they did.

By the 1870s, so many of the town's population regularly visited Soda Point that a collection was taken to build an eight-sided wooden pavilion, complete with a log roof, elaborately twisted wood hoops, and hitching racks for horses. The area was landscaped a bit to give it a more pleasing appearance, and the water was piped down from the rocks to make its retrieval less hazardous.

By the 1880s, the Soda Springs had become a virtual tourist attraction, with freighters stopping on the way to the mines in South Park and Leadville, and stagecoaches full of wide-eyed visitors and dignitaries. Public demand for this water was so great that in 1888 the city commissioned that a more permanent structure be built. Using inmate labor from the Territorial Prison – only a few short yards away, with a guard tower located atop the rocks above the springs – expert stone masons fashioned three beautiful red stone buildings. The large building in the center housed visitors as they enjoyed their refreshments. The small building to the left of the shelter enclosed the bubbling Soda Springs, and the small building to the right held the Iron Springs, which was fed from an iron pipe. Over the years, both springs were generally referred to as simply Soda Springs, or more formally, The Soda and Mineral Iron Springs.

To keep things in order, an inmate overseer was usually present to keep water glasses and the general area clean. He was also expected to tend to the warden's small cornfield and apple orchard only steps away.

Wooden pavilions covering the
Soda and Iron Springs, 1870.

The popularity of the Soda Springs continued to grow to the point where two local bottlers – Stockder and Lithia - attempted to bottle the water with syrup to make soda pop. Neither merchant was too successful, as the iron water quickly lost its fizz. But this failure did not deter the city from suggesting that the water had curative powers.

In the January 5, 1897 edition of the *Cañon City Clipper*, in an ongoing effort to promote Cañon City as a health resort, the writer makes the following claims:

"The Cold Springs – in Iron and Soda – which are located within the city, afford a great aid to digestion, and are beneficial in disorders of the liver and kidneys…"

Whether this reporter's claim had a basis of truth was irrelevant – and despite a years-long rumor that the Iron Springs was radioactive – droves of citizens and visitors continued to visit the Soda Springs regularly, until the popularity of automobiles in the 1920s and 1930s. The automobile carried locals and visitors to other nearby attractions. Still, the Soda Springs continued to be the place to congregate for those whose memories of love and affection – and childhood – were firmly connected to these waters.

Ward Collection

The Soda Springs, 1910.

That is, until 1949.

The Soda Springs was situated on land thought to be owned by the state of Colorado. In 1949, in a plan to widen U. S. Highway 50 at Soda Point, the State Highway Department needlessly demolished all three buildings at Soda Springs, and in the process, forever destroyed the flow of water. A public outcry ensued, but as there was little prior organized opposition, nothing could be done.

The Cañon City Lions Club later raised funds to redevelop the Soda Springs and pipe it to Veterans Memorial Park. But after much digging, all that was discovered was a trickle of water, and that was polluted by the water from an irrigation ditch that passed through a tunnel above the highway.

The original source of Soda Springs has never been found. All that remains are these photographs – and the wonderful, timeless memories of those who took pleasure in its natural state.

Ward Collection

Drinking from The Iron Springs, 1900.

Colorado Territorial Prison
275 W. Highway 50

In all cultures, civilized or otherwise, there always seems to be a collective method to handling those who do not fit within the standards set by these societies. The punishment for behavior outside accepted practices have included expulsion, shunning, public humiliation, torture, dismemberment, confinement, and even death.

For the wayfaring outlaw in Colorado in the nineteenth century, capture and conviction often meant the extreme of all punishments, or none at all.

Prior to the 1870s, the typical Colorado town's jail functioned more as an overnight dry-out facility for inebriated "guests," rather than a long-term confinement facility for felons. Rarely was a person held for more than a night or two, no matter the infraction alleged or conceded. Simply put, in spite of any legal conviction, there were no facilities within the territory to incarcerate prisoners for an extended period of time. Many outlaws who overstayed their welcome were either simply released – or hung from the nearest tree. Members of the Thirty-Ninth Congress grew alarmed by the growing rampant lawlessness in the Colorado Territory, and on June 22, 1867, approved expenditures for the construction of a penitentiary in the territory. It was up to the Legislature of the Territory to determine the location of the prison, but the cost of the prison could not exceed forty-thousand dollars.

Cañon City's newest legislator, attorney Thomas Macon, is generally credited for creating the drive that brought the penitentiary to the city. Typical today as it was then, Macon gained the support of other legislators for his bill to select Cañon City, by pledging his support for a bill to select Denver as the new capital city.

So it was that the Seventh Assembly of the Territorial Legislature awarded Cañon City the coveted designation. The resolution, however, specified that "...the site shall contain not less than twenty-five acres of land; the site so selected shall be conveyed to the Territory by the person or persons holding title thereto in fee simple absolutely without charge so as to vest title of same in the Territory." John Draper was the willing conveyor of that parcel of land at the southern foot of the hogbacks. In an ironic twist of fate, he apparently gave far more land than he had intended, and it took both an Act of the Territorial Legislature and an Act of Congress to return part of the land to him.

Inmates digging a water works system
at the Territorial Prison, 1880.

On January 1, 1871, the Territorial Prison was at last completed and opened. Built of native stone quarried from the nearby hillside, this three-story structure held thirty cells. U. S. Marshall Mark Shaffenberg acted as titular head, with Albert Walters as Chief Officer.

It was on January 13, 1871 that the first prisoner was received at the new facility. He was John Shepler, a butler from Gilpin County convicted of larceny and sentenced to one year of confinement. On the same day, William Henderson of Clear Creek County arrived for a five-year stay for manslaughter.

The first female prisoner was forty-two year old Mary Salander, who was also convicted of manslaughter, for which she was sentenced to three years. Rumor had it that Salander was also known as "Silver Heels," the famous Buckskin Joe dance hall girl who selflessly nursed dozens of miners and their families back to health during a smallpox epidemic. As inmate Number 60, Mary served less than five months of her sentence before being pardoned by the Governor in August of 1873.

In these early years, and for many decades thereafter, prison officers and guards wore blue uniforms with hard-billed caps. Inmates wore the very unpopular, but easily identifiable, striped clothing. One Denver newspaper reporter, in a feeble attempt to put a bright face on the prison's fashion failure, wrote that the inmates were "attired in white woolen suits which were handsomely decorated with black stripes."

In April of 1874, the Territorial Prison was conveyed by the U. S. Government to the Territory of Colorado. Thus began a long, uneasy history of the prison playing host to a seemingly endless number of wardens, beginning with pioneer Anson Rudd, who lasted barely three months in the post. The prison staff, who were paid twenty-five dollars per month, included four day shift guards, and two night shift guards. By 1899, the number of staff had grown considerably, along with the number of cell houses (3), and the number of inmates (582), with the addition of a large stone wall surrounding the facility. The deputy warden's house was added in 1901, as was the administration building in 1910. It was at the administration building that the Prison Band would gather on the balcony and play for the public in the park below.

Today, very little of the original facility of 1870 remains. "Old Max," as it is now called, continues to function as a penitentiary, having gone through multiple renovations and re-buildings throughout the past century. Most of State Park, which was located directly opposite the front entrance to the prison, is mostly a parking lot these days. Main Street, which ran just a few feet from the south prison wall, was rerouted to Royal Gorge Boulevard. The public can no longer listen to the Prison

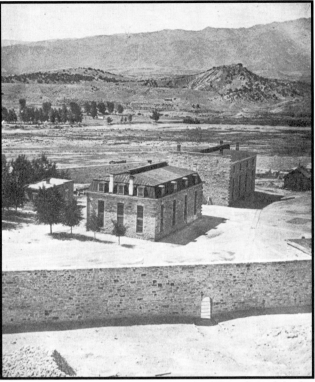

Local History Center, Cañon City

Territorial Prison in 1878
with its first stone wall.

Local History Center, Cañon City

Prison yard, 1880. Person with arms
folded (far left) is Barney McCowan.

Band playing from the balcony on warm Sunday afternoons, nor can they drink from the water at Soda Springs just west of the prison grounds.

Although much of the history of the early days of the Territorial Prison – when it served to house mostly outlaws of the old West – has been lost, the museum on prison grounds does offer visitors a glimpse of what prison life was like back in the nineteenth century.

This is a photograph of the Territorial Prison in 1912 when Main Street
extended well beyond the prison - but only steps away from the prison's main gates.
Note the abundance of trees along Main Street, with State Park in the immediate
righthand portion of the picture.

George Witherell
And
Frontier Justice

To the probable chagrin of many of Cañon City's founding fathers, the tale of George Witherell remains an indelible part of the town's history and lore. While the Royal Gorge and Skyline Drive are the areas most revered by visitors to this historic city, the life and death of George Witherell is as much a part of Cañon City's legacy as a Wild West town.

In 1871, at the age of twenty-two years, George Witherell was convicted of murdering a Douglas County, Colorado man by gunshot, then hacking him to pieces with an axe and stealing his possessions. There must have been doubt in the minds of the jurors, as he received a life sentence, rather than death by hanging. He was sent to Cañon City's newly built Colorado Territorial Penitentiary. He was inmate number 23.

Two years into his sentence, Witherell escaped from prison. He hid in the nearby mountains for twenty days until his eventual capture. When he was returned he was beaten and placed in solitary confinement. Other, similar incidents ensued, and frequently he found himself confined in both arm and leg shackles.

An educated and literate man who wrote in a Spencerian hand, and despite his numerous attempts to escape prison, George found a sympathetic ear in Warden Felton. The Warden was quoted as saying that "Feelings were running high between cattle and sheep men, and while I never entertained that Witherell was innocent, it appeared to me that the murder was the result of intense feelings at the time." He further stated that he believed that George had "lived an honest, honorable life."

Warden Felton made his thoughts known to Governor Adams, and in April of 1888, after fifteen years of confinement, George Witherell was released on a pardon. He quickly found work doing odd jobs, mostly in Pueblo and Colorado Springs. But he grew restless. He quickly learned that ex-convicts had difficulty trusting others, and being trusted. And then he met one Charles McCain.

Charles McCain was a young rancher and freighter from Beaver Creek, and along with his young bride, was hoping to start a moving business in Cañon City. It was now October of 1888, and Witherell apparently convinced McCain that he could help him fulfill his dreams. But when McCain's wife soon received a letter from her husband stating that he was selling his wagons and horses, she grew alarmed and summoned the law. A posse was formed and the group soon caught up with

Stern-faced townsfolk posing with the
lifeless body of George Witherell,
December 4, 1888.

A sheriff's posse gathered at Fifth and Main Streets, 1888.
Quite possibly the same posse that tracked George Witherell to Denver.

Witherell and McCain's wagons at Gouldings Stables on the outskirts of Denver. The next day they found the lifeless body of twenty-four year old Charles McCain in a ravine near Turkey Creek. He had been shot in the head and hacked with an axe. Witherell loudly declared his innocence, but to no avail. He was taken to a jail in Denver to await his fate.

Fremont County Sheriff Morgan Griffith heard angry talk fomenting amongst the citizenry about Witherell's likelihood of surviving the ride back to Cañon City to stand trial. He wisely decided it might be best to wait a few days before attempting such a journey.

Some two months later, when tempers subsided and angry talk had declined, the sheriff quietly made his long trek to Denver alone, and quickly returned with his prisoner to the county jail near First and Greenwood Streets just before midnight. It was December 3rd, and the simple horse and buggy made hardly a sound as they approached the jail. The sheriff thought he had made the return undetected, but within an hour, a small group of men knocked on the jailhouse door and demanded that he turn over his prisoner. When Griffith refused, the group suddenly turned into an angry mob and threatened harm to the sheriff. At that point, Griffith drew two pistols and offered to shoot the first man to enter the jail. None obliged, and the crowd dispersed.

At about 3:00 a.m. on December 4th, there was a soft knock on the door of the jail. When the very tired and drowsy sheriff unhooked the latch, he was overwhelmed by two large masked men. Suddenly the jail was filled with a dozen masked men, and the sheriff was bound and carted away unharmed.

Fremont County's first jail where George Witherell was held. It still stands at 104 Greenwood Avenue.

George Witherell, if nothing else, was an attentive listener to all that transpired since his late arrival that night. Anticipating an ugly reception, he had torn a leg off his wooden bed and fashioned a makeshift club. When the masked men entered his cell they were met with curses and hard blows to the head. Suddenly a shot rang out, and George's left arm went limp from a wound in his left shoulder. No longer able to defend himself, he was dragged to a telegraph pole at First and Main – where the State Armory now stands – and was quickly and unceremoniously lynched.

Interestingly, a coroner's jury wrote that Witherell's death came from a person or persons unknown. Even the sheriff claimed he could not determine who had bound and gagged him that night. Further, of all the articles written about George Witherell at that time, and since, not one questioned whether he might actually have been innocent of the charges against him.

But the story does not end here.

Whatever happened to George Witherell's body? This is one mystery that no one has yet to completely solve. It is known that a local pharmacist removed his brain to see if it was of normal size (it was), then pickled it in a bathtub and charged admission to those desiring to view it. Another enterprising fellow even lopped off Witherell's upper lip in order to display his impressively large handlebar mustache – along with his suspenders, part of the rope that hung him, his mustache comb, four spent cartridges, and a photo of the lynching. All were framed and hung in the lobby of a local hotel for many years.

But where are the remains of George Witherell?

From Fruit Days To Blossom Festivals
Main Street

It has long been a tradition in small towns all across America to acknowledge new growing seasons or harvests through community celebrations that are part festive and part commerce-based. This tradition actually predates American history by thousands of years, with similar such celebrations by the ancient Greeks, Egyptians, and Chinese, and many other cultures long since disappeared. But in small towns like ours, that history is not altogether relevant, because the sun sets and rises on the accomplishments and achievements of the individuals in these towns, making each community unique and profoundly different.

Cañon City has never been shy about showing unbridled exuberance for its festivals and fairs. To this end, the town has always loved a parade, and its parades have always been a microcosm of the town at large, from the fire fighting hose teams of the 1890s, to the high school bands of the 1990s. From the beginning of the town's history, and always complete with an impressive array of delicacies from funnel cakes to candy apples, parades have always bared the town's soul.

The first recorded mention of a festival in Cañon City occurred in the 1860s in the *Cañon City Times*. By the 1880s, residents were celebrating Fruit Day as both an acknowledgement of their remarkable harvests, and a way to acquaint neighboring communities with their bountiful products. The 1890s found Fruit Day being organized by the Fremont County Horticultural Society, with as many as ten thousand annual visitors enjoying this one-day event. They came primarily by passenger train from such far off places as Denver, Colorado Springs, La Junta, and Rocky Ford. Paper plates filled with apples, plums, pears, peaches and grapes were given away to all visitors. The fruit was displayed in grand fashion in a large fifty-foot pavilion on Main Street, and in a delicate manner at the opera house. The *Rocky Mountain News* held that sixteen tons of fruit were distributed in 1894 alone.

For many years, tours of the Territorial Prison were conducted with as many as five thousand gawkers passing through its gates. A like number also toured the orchards of Rockafellow, Harrison, Catlin, Trout and others into the areas of Fruitmere, Orchard Park, Park Center and Lincoln Park. And when the day was done, visitors did not immediately return to their home cities, but stayed with residents in makeshift boarding houses and campgrounds, and in the town's few available hotel rooms.

Ward Collection

Fruit Pyramid, 1895.

Fruit Day in Cañon City continued until about 1900 when it was then called May Day, shifting the emphasis from harvest to blossom. The orchard tours continued, but were now at the beginning of the planting season. Local fruit farmers and the nurserymen had effectively gotten the word out about this garden city's produce, and were now disinclined to give away their products for nothing.

It is believed that the first use of the word "blossom" in relation to the annual celebration was coined by wealthy Cañon City resident Dall DeWeese, who entertained several dozen friends at his home during a May Day event in 1908 that he termed "blossom fete." His home was decorated with thousands of fruit blossoms and lilacs. So popular was this gathering that the guest list the following year rose to over one hundred guests.

By the time 1910 arrived, DeWeese's private affair had turned into a public gathering and renamed the Flower Carnival, complete with a May pole dance, flower queen (Miss Lillie Ruhndahl) and music from both the Cañon City High School and Territorial Prison bands.

Local History Center, Cañon City

The Cañon City Fire Department parades through
town during the 1911 Flower Carnival.

Miss Cherry, a questionable name for this lovely young lady
in the 1921 Blossom Day Parade.

Two years later, in 1912, the blossom celebrations were under the direction of the Cañon City Improvement League, and by 1913 it was being called the Blossom Day Celebration. In addition to managing the celebration, the League also coordinated an annual city clean-up project in preparation for the welcoming of the town's annual visitors.

The World War I years almost brought an end to the Blossom Day events. With the war raging in Europe, and emphasis clearly focused on the war effort, the League decided not to promote the event outside of the city. These festivals were marked by low attendance, but enthusiastic local participation. After the war, the Cañon City Chamber of Commerce began sponsoring the event and attendance once again began to skyrocket, with five thousand people traveling to the city each spring from 1926 to 1937. The Boy Scouts were information directors, baseball games at the Abbey were in vogue, and an airplane ride over the orchards was the new popular attraction.

The year of 1938 saw the first Jaycees-sponsored Blossom Festival. With a well-coordinated publicity campaign, attendance ballooned to eight thousand people. The following year of 1939 also marked the very first Band Festival Day, with bands from all across the state competing for the coveted trophies. And the 1940 event brought ten thousand visitors for a carnival, a dance at the Annex, boxing at the State Armory, and, of course, the highly anticipated parade down Main Street.

Once again, the war years of the 1940s compelled the Jaycees to sponsor what they referred to as "token" blossom festivals. With little publicity, the resulting turnouts were predictably well-below normal. However, after the war, participation returned greater than ever, and by 1948 more than thirty-five thousand visitors made a rousing return to Cañon City. Since that time, the Jaycees-sponsored Blossom Festival has consistently been Cañon City's longest and best attended event in the city's history.

1937 July 4th parade on Main Street.

CANON CITY SOFTBALL
OPENING NIGHT MONDAY JUNE 6

1937 Blossom Festival parade float.

The Flour Mills of Cañon City
100 Block of Main Street

As the son of an East Tennessee farmer, I would take great pleasure in accompanying my father to the local mill to pick up a sack or two of locally grown and milled grain. The fresh smell of cracked corn, laying mash and wheat could be overwhelming to the senses. There is something powerful and pure and natural about the scent of sacked grain; it settles the spirit and brings us back to the simpler times we knew in our youth. Although my late father and I stopped being farmers too long ago, I am still drawn by the lure of a simple sack of grain at Frontier Feeds, and the feel of flour and corn meal as it passes through my fingers. That feeling is often understood as a cleansing of the soul – as it probably was for the pioneers who first milled grain in Fremont County.

After the first settlers began arriving in Cañon City around 1859, the first crops planted were corn and wheat. It is believed that Lewis Conley of the lower Beaver Creek settlement built the first mill to process the harvests for local use. Not long thereafter, Colonel E. Johnson and Egbert Bradley built their mill in the Four Mile area on Four Mile Creek in 1864.

George Rockafellow, an experienced miller, arrived in Cañon City in the same year of the building of the Four Mile mill. An enterprising and confident fellow, he was immediately hired to manage the mill and did so for the four years it operated at this location.

In 1868, Rockafellow took charge in building a newer and larger mill within city limits at First and Second Streets at the south side of Main Street, which was named the Cañon City Mill. A three-story wood frame building, the mill was powered by the water from the Mill Ditch. This mill was operated successfully and profitably for the next sixteen years, until it quickly burned to the ground in 1884. By this time Rockafellow had moved on, becoming Cañon City's first mayor in 1872, and eventually to build his vast holdings in agriculture in the Fruitmere area.

Less than two years after the fire, early settler W. J. Wilson, who had little experience in milling, decided to rebuild the mill at the same location. He saw that Johnson and Bradley did well financially, and he believed an opportunity for continuing a milling operation in Cañon City made good business sense. Wilson's hunch was correct. The Cañon City Mill, as he continued to call it, was rebuilt in 1886 and Wilson successfully operated it until 1908, when he sold it to J. O. Stearns. Stearns was involved in a number of other local firms. He soon lost interest in the mill and quickly sold it to U. E. Sidebottom, but before doing so, he installed new milling equipment and machinery.

Local History Center, Cañon City

Main Street, Cañon City. The morning after
the 1915 fire that leveled the Peerless Flour Mill.

It is evident that U. E. Sidebottom had a solid business plan in place when he bought the mill. Not content to serve just local flour needs, he looked beyond the borders of Fremont County for the distribution of his product. He named his new operation Peerless Flour Company, and with Kentucky red wheat, began furnishing stores with his Peerless Flour. By 1912, the company was shipping flour not only all over Colorado, but also to many neighboring states. But more importantly, Sidebottom was able to secure a large contract with the U. S. Government to provide flour for the Ute Indians of Colorado.

Regionally, the Peerless Company fearlessly competed with the larger milling firms in Kansas, eventually gaining comparable rail shipping rates all across the country. This allowed Peerless to market their own brands of flour to stores nationwide. Brands of flour such as Peerless, Our Special, Jessie O, and On Time quickly became recognizable and highly sought-after products.

In 1913, the Peerless Flour Company building was struck by lightning, but sustained little damage. The incident was considered a minor setback.

However, late on the evening of November 17, 1915, the Peerless Mill was completely destroyed by fire, most likely the result of a spark from a faulty electrical motor. Starting in the east end of the mill, the fire spread quickly, igniting tons of sacks of wheat, oats and flour. Before long, the machinery and stored grain collapsed through the floors and into the basement area, shooting flames that could be seen for miles. The fire was not extinguished until the dawn of the following morning.

The Peerless Flour Mill was never rebuilt, effectively ending the almost fifty-year history of milling flour in Cañon City.

The Strathmore Hotel
331 Main Street

Cañon City was still considered a simple pioneer village in 1872, with mostly log cabins, and only a few short years removed from the time that only Anson Rudd and a few others comprised the town's only residents.

But 1872 was also the year that William H. McClure began construction of a large brick hotel building on the edge of town at the corner of Fourth and Main Streets. A wealthy investor, McClure had constructed the first frame building in Cañon City, as well as several other commercial buildings. But this building was different. It was meant to be a hotel that would rival the best modern hotels in the East.

On land that originally held Rudd's long log blacksmith shop, McClure began the two year building project using brick manufactured locally. This imposing three-story structure also had a then-unusual addition – a basement. With a strong cement foundation, the purpose of the basement was to house enough space for below-ground shops, which were to be illuminated by street level skylights of amethyst glass.

The hotel was opened in grand fashion on the evening of October 4, 1874, and ably dubbed "McClure House" after its builder. Mayor Thomas Macon offered the dedication, followed by his wife, Mary Macon, in a piano recital. Anson Rudd, Sr. read a poem he had written for the event, while an orchestra entertained in the lobby. Hundreds of candles were placed in the windows of the hotel's seventy rooms, providing an elegant spectacle never before seen by residents. The *Cañon City Times* reported that, "... a brilliant scene was presented which could be seen from afar, and was gazed upon in admiration by many people. Children gazed in wonder at the lighted building, which had never seen a sight of that character, having been raised on the frontier, where such sights are not of frequent occurrence. The people gathered in, and, by 8 o'clock, the large double parlor doors and spacious halls were peopled by a happy throng. All agreed the building was a model of its kind – spacious, well-lighted and ventilated."

Mrs. Maria M. Sheetz was the first manager of the hotel. A cultured and refined individual, Mrs. Sheetz was a retired Illinois school teacher who had earlier traveled to Cañon City to manage the Fremont House at First and Main Streets. This location is now occupied by the vintage Territorial Prison's Deputy Warden's home.

Mrs. Sheetz leased the McClure House from William McClure, and it was she who set the tone and sophisticated atmosphere that set it apart from other establishments. She purchased all of the hotel's furnishings from shops in Denver, and leased space in the basement to a barber shop, a hardware store, and a paint shop. The barber shop, in particular, was lauded as being the finest west of St. Louis. She also leased a portion of the hotel to Fred Raynolds for his Fremont County Bank, until he built his own Raynolds Bank Building across the street.

With sixty sleeping rooms, three suites, and ten bathrooms, the McClure House was the most visited hotel in the territory, and clearly one of Cañon City's best investments. Concord Stagecoach drivers stopped at the hotel for refreshment. Actors and politicians alike stayed at the hotel, although it was often difficult to tell them apart. A popular attraction was the hotel's pristine restaurant, which attracted many satisfied diners.

In August of 1900, the McClure House was sold to a group of English investors, who renamed it The Strathmore Hotel. One of the new owners was thought to be the Earl of Strathmore, and for many years the family crest was prominently displayed above the hotel's massive fireplace. A quiet but ornate reading room was added, and many sleeping rooms were renovated at a cost of twelve thousand dollars. Included in that sum were new velvet carpets, white iron beds with brass fittings, and furniture made of mahogany, birch, maple and oak.

Long revered for its role in the growth and development of Cañon City, it is believed that the Strathmore Hotel was Colorado's longest continuously operated hotel by the time it closed in 1981. It was there almost from the town's earliest beginnings; it has hosted both the famous and the infamous, and it continues to lend a commanding physical presence to today's downtown.

The Strathmore Hotel is also a place of mystery and a place of interest, because within the walls of this historic hotel are generations of stories that have yet to be told.

The Strathmore Hotel, 1922.

The Fremont County Farm & Hospital
3250 E. Main Street
(U. S. Highway 50 East)

To those who knew better, it was degradingly called "The Poor Farm." To those who lived there, it was home.

By design, the Fremont County Farm and Hospital was a way-station for the sick, neglected and the injured, and a home for those who were too young or too old to care for themselves.

Jesse Rader had a small farm on Four Mile Creek that he sold to the county in October of 1865 for $1,925. The county kept a section of the farmhouse and built a new Fremont County Hospital in 1876 to replace one that had burned to the ground. The burned hospital was known as "The Pest House," a place that no one ever visited willingly. This deplorable canvas-roofed hospital had twenty small cots. It was little more than a warehouse for those unable to afford medical attention, regular hospitalization, or suffered from communicable diseases, such as smallpox or scarlet fever. When the building burned, there were few mourners.

It was in 1900 that the county appointed its first superintendent to oversee the management of the County Farm and Hospital. With forty beds, it was everything that The Pest House was not. Persons of every age – from newborns to one person aged ninety-seven years – were guests at the farm. Transients injured while jumping from moving train cars were frequent temporary guests, as were the temporarily unemployed who worked the dairy farm or orchard to earn their board. Some stayed overnight, others for years.

To the young, the innocent, and those uninitiated to the ways of the world, the County Farm became home by way of parental neglect, abuse, abandonment, or simply because they had nowhere else to go. The first resident of record was "Minnie Silby, age 10. No friends or parents." One young nine-year-old boy became a years-long resident because he was "too young to earn a living." Still other children came because of death or illness of both parents. Some were sent to an orphanage in Denver, while others simply ran away.

History teaches that the best years of our lives are our childhood years. We can only imagine the sense of fear, uncertainty and lack of personal security these children must have felt in their younger days, undoubtedly, feelings that followed them well into adulthood.

Initially, for the first few years, patients and guests were referred to as inmates. By the late 1920s that terminology changed when the hospital was updated to rival the best hospitals in southern Colorado. Suddenly, inmates became patients, and the older residents needing long term care became guests, especially after pensions began paying as much as $95 a month for board.

In time, conditions changed and the world changed, and our definition of social services changed with it. The County Farm and Hospital closed in 1973, after ninety-seven years of dedicated service to the poor, sick, homeless, neglected, abused and aged.

The two and three story Queen Anne style buildings at the complex were dismantled in 1996, and the giant cottonwood trees that surrounded the hospital were reduced to firewood. Nothing remains today of the Fremont County Farm and Hospital.

Local History Center, Cañon City

Fremont County Farm and Hospital, 1922.

Mack's Lumber Yard
531 Main Street

This small plot of land was originally occupied in 1870 as a large corral for horses and freight wagons transporting much needed supplies to Cripple Creek, Leadville, and the Wet Mountain Valley. By 1875, Mack and Kennedy formed a partnership and built a lumber yard opposite the Sartor Livery Stables. When the partnership dissolved in 1877, sole owner Henry Mack renamed the business Mack's Lumber Yard. When Henry died in 1882, his heirs eventually sold the yard in 1890 and it became Newton Lumber Company.

The ground at 531 Main Street remained a lumber yard until 1902, when George A. Baker and C. A. Biggs built a two-story brick and concrete building and named it the Baker & Biggs building. In the dry goods, clothing, and carpet business (The Favorite Dry Goods Emporium), the proprietors also rented out the upstairs offices to physician Dr. W. T. Little, and dentist Dr. F. A. Twitchell.

The Baker & Biggs building was touted as the most modern building in the region, with one of the first elevators – installed by Nowels Mercantile Co. – and a sales staff of eleven employees. The business was so well respected that they even developed a prosperous mail order branch of the store.

By 1913, Baker & Biggs sold out to the Nowels Mercantile Co., at which time the store was then being called the Nowels-Stockton Mercantile Company. In turn, they transferred ownership of the building to the First National Bank in 1917. The bank moved into the corner spot of 531 Main Street, but rented out addresses 527 and 529 to other merchants, such as J. C. Penney in 1918, and Thomas Hardware in 1937. The bank eventually took over the entire building in 1966.

The interior of the bank was completely remodeled in 1928, to the extent that the old steel teller cages were removed and sold to a San Luis Valley bank. Later remodeling occurred in 1948, 1968, and in 1991.

Local History Center, Cañon City

Mack's Lumber Yard, 1880.

Local History Center, Cañon City

Baker & Biggs Building, 1922.

The Hanging Bridge
The Royal Gorge

The story goes that a few years back a former Pennsylvanian, who had recently relocated to Cañon City, was invited to view the Royal Gorge from atop the Suspension Bridge. Amazed by what he saw, and with little urging, he proceeded to ride down the Incline Railway to enjoy the raging waters of the Arkansas River firsthand. Upon arrival he looked to his left and saw a mass of V-shaped steel girders and cables and asked what it was. His companion replied that it was the Hanging Bridge. By now wide-eyed and his jaw-dropping, he squinted, then asked, "Who got hung there?"

By virtue of Cañon City's Wild West reputation for vigilante justice, the Hanging Bridge has probably been the unintentional butt of similar misunderstandings since its construction in 1879. Although no one knows for certain how the bridge received its unofficial moniker, the name nevertheless stuck. While the bridge can also accurately be referred to as an elevated or above-ground bridge, these and all other names were summarily rejected by both locals and visitors alike. Thus it remains today as simply the Hanging Bridge.

In the1870s, when the railroads were scouting for a passage to lay track along the Arkansas through the Royal Gorge, they noticed that the walls of the canyon narrowed to only forty feet wide right in the middle of the gorge. With solid granite walls rising a thousand feet on both sides of the river, attempting to lay track was first thought to be risky, foolhardy, and next to impossible. However, A. A. Robinson, chief engineer for the Santa Fe Railroad, hired St. Louis engineer and bridge builder Charles Shaler Smith to design a structure that could support the colossal weight of a fully-loaded train.

Within days of arriving at the Royal Gorge, Smith devised an unheard of plan of supporting the inside rail of track on a masonary ledge running almost three hundred feet, with the outside rail hanging from massive steel girders that were imbedded into the walls of the canyon.

Charles Shaler Smith's bridge design was an instant and overwhelming success. At a cost of twelve thousand dollars, the completed Hanging Bridge won worldwide acclaim as one of the most improbable engineering accomplishments of its time. It became such a popular attraction that all passenger trains through the canyon stopped for a few minutes during each run so that the passengers

Charles Shaler Smith and assistants surveying
the site of the proposed Hanging Bridge, 1878.

The nearly completed Hanging Bridge, 1879.

Local History Center, Cañon City

The first passenger train through the Royal Gorge, 1879.

Local History Center, Cañon City

The AT and SF locomotive No. 1, Echo, was the first engine through the Royal Gorge in 1879. On the box at the rear of the engine, it reads: "Profile & Franconia Notch."

could have their photographs taken at the bridge. In the early years those passengers included dignitaries such as Teddy Roosevelt, Supreme Court Chief Justice Earl Warren, and the entire 1910 Chicago White Sox baseball team.

Ward Collection

The Hanging Bridge, 1901.

Law Kee's Chinese Laundry
606 Main Street

Chinese immigration to the United States in the nineteenth century was one fraught with great promise, unlimited opportunity, violence, and finally, exclusion.

In 1850, there were about four thousand Chinese living and working in the United States. With the sudden discovery of gold in California and the Southwest, the number of Chinese arrivals increased to an unbelievable twenty thousand by 1852. Because of the drought in the Canton Province in China between 1847 to 1850, the forced open door policy following the infamous Opium Wars of 1839 to 1842, the Taiping Rebellion of 1851 to 1864, and many, many political considerations, the United States of America became the land of opportunity for many Chinese workers eager to start new lives abroad.

Early on, Chinese workers were recruited to work the gold mines in California, Colorado, Nevada, Oregon, Montana and South Dakota. By the late 1850s, thousands were contracted to build the Transcontinental Railroad, often laying as much as ten miles of track a day. When the tracks were finished, many workers stayed in the railroad towns and started new businesses, or hired on as laborers or farm workers.

In the 1870s, the first indications of discrimination arose when labor groups warned that Chinese labor would eventually overtake all jobs in the East. Soon Chinese laundries appeared in many Eastern cities, having already been established in Colorado, California, and Montana. In Colorado, specifically, Chinese miners were also hired as strikebreakers, fomenting an already growing resentment against them. And soon thereafter, nine thousand of the ten thousand Chinese workers who built the Union Pacific Railroad were fired after being perceived as threatening the job security of non-Asian workers.

In the beginning, because of the sudden national labor shortage, and the advancements due to the industrial revolution that opened factories and mills, the Chinese were welcomed with open arms by Americans. But by the early 1880s, the doors were shut tightly after protests of anti-Chinese slogans and frequent violence ensued. Many Chinese were assaulted, killed, or driven from the towns in which they worked. Locally, the bias was evident in other ways. In one local newspaper, the writer, promoting a non-Asian laundry, states that the owner "has paid out in salaries the sum of $8,000 – over $2,600 a year – and if he had the business that is divided up

Local History Center, Cañon City

Law Kee, 1881.

among the Chinamen (who, by the way, are in no wise a desirable commodity in any community), his pay roll would easily be doubled."

Law Kee was one of the "Chinamen" referenced in that newspaper article. Judging from the setting and quality of the photograph of Law Kee, and his attire, this is a picture of a successful businessman. There is little doubt he would have sent photographs to relatives to express his good fortune. In time, however, economics and discrimination drove him back to his home city of Silver Cliff, never to return. The year after this 1881 photograph was taken, President Chester A. Arthur signed into law the Chinese Exclusion Act, which stopped the immigration of skilled and unskilled Chinese laborers into the United States. The law was not repealed until 1943.

The building at 606 Main Street that housed Law Kee's Chinese Laundry was razed around 1900. The site would later become the home of the Jones Motion Picture Company, now Skyline Theatre.

Local History Center, Cañon City

The occasion is the laying of the cornerstone for the Masonic Temple.
The building housing Law Kee's Chinese Laundry is located
in the upper lefthand portion of this photograph, 1880.

The Palace Drug Store
401 Main Street

The typical drug store of a hundred years ago offered not only medicinal remedies for physical and mental ailments, but was also the local center for the purchase of elegant writing paper, cigars, and hair products. But to many eager youngsters, the drug store was the best place to sit at the counter and slowly sip a ten-cent concoction of soda water thick with syrup. It was also the best place for a young fellow to take his best girl for a sundae after a performance at the opera house, or a show at the Jones Theatre.

Cañon City has almost always had a drug store, and while many have come and gone, it seems the Palace Drug Store has been with us from the very beginning – long before the taking of the accompanying photograph.

Initially named Merriam & Pedley Drugs in the 1880s, the original store was located on the south side of the 400 block of Main Street. By the end of the century, George Pedley bought out Merriam, moved the store to 401 Main Street, and changed the store's name to Palace Drug.

By 1902, Pedley sold his interest in the store to two Florence druggists, Alf R. Mitchell and Lloyd Egbers. The store was then moved to its present location at 601 Main Street in 1907, where it continues to thrive today.

The building at 401 Main Street was first constructed in 1879 by Theodore Marsh Harding and brother Lebbeus L. Harding. It has housed many of Cañon City's early businesses, such as Harding Hardware Store, Beecher's Drug, Palau Drug Store, City Grocery & Market, and for many years, the popular café and bar, The Shanty.

Local History Center, Cañon City

Merriam & Pedley Drugs, C. 1882.

Rocky Mountain Bakery
414 Main Street

Imagine the rich, heavy aroma of freshly baked breads and pastries rising from the modest ovens of this bakery. Large, thick loaves of wheat bread from flour milled locally, or the now-forgotten taste of salt-rising bread, coupled with the mouth-watering pies and sweet rolls – all could be detected with little effort many blocks away. Such was the nature of a neighborhood bakery. And such was the life of the Rocky Mountain Bakery.

Between 1880 and 1920, bakeries in Cañon City came and went with alarming regularity, seeming to exist no more than a year or two, at best. But Riede's Rocky Mountain Bakery was an exception.

Fred Riede started one of the first bakeries in Cañon City in 1880, and the Riede legacy lasted more than thirty years. This was an unheard of length of time in a changing, evolving frontier town. Known for his breads, cakes and pies, Riede also offered an extensive line of tobaccos, cigars, and soda water.

Although the Rocky Mountain Bakery name is prominently displayed above the shop window in this photograph, Riede's bakeries also took the names of The California Bakery, Riede's Bakery, and Fred Riede Bakery and Confectionery.

The building at 414 Main Street was constructed in 1887. It was also the home of L. Mann Company Bakery & Confectionery (1903), Dillon Bakery (bought by E. E. Riede in 1904), The Ott Candy Company (1907), The Alice Brodham Beckham Hat Shop (1918), Hays Millinery (1918), and more recently, the Regalia Flower Shop, and since 1994, Cañon Framing and Décor.

Riede's Rocky Mountain Bakery, 1905.

City Park
West River Street Park
Veterans Memorial Park
Royal Gorge Boulevard

Anyone who has ever taken a slow walk through a tree-lined park during a warm spring afternoon, or arrived early and watched the light shine through the trees when morning breaks, deeply understands how important a park can be to a town's well-being.

In a literal sense, whether in a conscious one or not, parks are generally designed and built to add civility to an often uncivilized setting, to approximate nature at its best, while eliminating those aspects – dead trees, weeds, and fallen branches – that the human eye deems unsightly. As essentially agrarians, we are strangely drawn to the bright colorful flowers that are planted there, and we silently revel in their existence. It is at that very same moment that we are at our very best.

City Park, which has owned several different names, was not always the idyllic setting that we see today. This area of five and one-half acres was originally owned by the Cañon City Water Company. The city acquired this parcel of land in 1881 and named it West River Street Park. West River Street once ran through a quiet residential neighborhood. The street was widened in the 1960s and renamed Royal Gorge Boulevard. Many of the homes on the street were removed, but the park area remained.

In its early day as a park, the city constructed a bandstand that served as a beautiful setting for performances by local community musical groups. It was especially utilized for Fruit Day and Labor Day celebrations. As can be seen by these photographs, the park had a pristine appearance that rivaled the immaculate parks of Denver.

By the 1930s, the West River Street Park's name had been shortened to the more easily remembered and generic "City Park." The bandstand had deteriorated and was removed. Although never referred to as a "Hooverville," the park did acquire the name of "Tent City," as it served as a central location for the large number of individuals and families who were hard hit by the county's economic depression.

In the ensuing years, and until 1956, City Park earned the unflattering nickname of "Hollywood Flats." It was the setting for many circuses, carnivals and other traveling shows of every kind. In

City Park, 1916.

addition, the city also used the area as a site for mixing road paving materials and to store heavy equipment.

By the early 1950s, City Park was an eyesore and an embarrassment to the entire community. Under the astute leadership of U. Michael Welch, a Citizen's Advisory Committee was formed to study ways to improve the park's appearance.

Since the city did not have funds available for the upkeep of the park, the Citizen's Committee devised an ambitious plan that centered around a volunteer day known as "C Day." The goal was to construct a brand new park in a single day.

On April 21, 1956, more than two hundred men, women, and children, with pickup trucks, dump trucks, shovels and front-end loaders, eagerly started work on the park by removing oil-soaked soil and replacing it with ten-thousand yards of fresh dirt from South Cañon. Numerous businesses donated food and beverages for these volunteers, and other groups prepared these meals.

By the day's end, City Park had been completely transformed. The ground had been seeded and trees planted. In years to follow, picnic tables, restrooms, an amphitheatre, a fountain and a playground were added – and, again, the name of the park was changed. It was now being called Veterans Memorial Park, as it remains today. It is, once again, the pride of the community.

Yes, a city park can be, and often is, the best that nature can offer, even in unnatural settings.

City Park, 1910.

The Fremont County Courthouse
100 Block Of Macon Avenue
Fourth Street And Macon Avenue

It was hailed as the last courthouse Fremont County would ever need. As the county's first official courthouse, it almost did not last half a decade.

When talk of a need for a county courthouse began in the early 1870s, the county commissioners finally supported a bond issue that voters approved. At thirty thousand dollars, a magnificent brick and stone building was constructed by July of 1881. The cost included the land (part of which was donated by the Colorado Coal & Iron Company,) a stone wall and iron railing fronting the complex, office furnishings, and a few planted trees. Residents were overjoyed by the handsome and imposing building, believing it to be the finest structure in all of Colorado.

However, elation was short-lived. Within only a few months of the building's completion, the foundation began to sink; walls cracked and plaster fell from the ceilings, and of greater alarm, the hallways suddenly appeared "wavy," as if having suffered damage in an earthquake. The commissioners sought the advice of a Denver architect, who suggested inserting iron rods into the foundation walls. It didn't help. Nothing the commissioners tried could stop the sinking and eventual collapse of the building.

Nothing, that is, except one final, desperate plan.

In April of 1886, after almost five difficult years battling the town's largest sinkhole, the beautiful courthouse at the 100 Block of Macon Avenue was carefully dismantled – brick by brick – and reassembled at the corner of Fourth Street and Macon Avenue. This property was owned by Fremont County Bank President Fred Raynolds, who sold it to the county for $2,300. The stonework, bricks, window frames, wood interior and all other parts were delicately detached, numbered, and reinstalled at the new location. The building's impressive clock tower and one-ton bell were lowered into a wagon and painstakingly placed back atop the building after it was reconstructed.

But where did the county's employees go during this time? They were hastily relocated to rented space in the Harding Block building at Fourth and Main Streets during the transition.

By January of 1888, after one year and nine months of faithful labor, at an additional cost of twenty thousand dollars, the deed was finally done and county employees slowly began moving back into the relocated building. The structure faithfully served the county's needs until 1961, when a

Fremont County Courthouse,
100 Block of Macon Avenue, 1882.

less visually impressive county courthouse was built at the 600 Block of Macon Avenue at a cost of two million dollars.

The old courthouse was finally razed in 1965. Other than the weather vane (which was donated to the Florence Museum) the only part of the building that was saved was the large thirty-foot clock tower, which was given to the Cañon City Municipal Museum. Inoperable since 1959, the Edward Howard & Co. Clock was eventually repaired by Jim Cole of Silver Cliff. In 2005, this historic clock found a new home at the corner of Third and Main Streets.

Fremont County Courthouse,
Fourth Street & Macon Avenue, 1920.

Junior Reserve Officer Training Corps
Cañon City High School

High school military training was first formally established in Cañon City in 1881. The Colorado Collegiate & Military Institute opened a three-story school building at Seventh and Pike Streets, in the same location that later became home to St. Scholastica Academy. The brainchild of E. H. Sawyer, a Union Army Civil War veteran, the school for both boys and girls offered instruction in subjects such as art, philosophy, languages, literature, engineering, and, of course, military training. The school published its own newspaper in 1882, *The Cadet*, with the assistance of new teacher Frederick Bonfils, who later became editor and publisher of the *Denver Post*.

The military school closed in December of 1885, and military training was not again offered to high school students in the area until 1901.

T. B. Coulter, president of the Cañon City school board in 1901, is generally credited with leading the campaign to add military training to the high school curriculum. By 1913, it had become a required course of study for all four-year high school students. It was not until 1932 that it became an elective for junior and seniors, but still required for freshmen and sophomores. Training entailed close order drills and practice hikes with full field packs. Students were issued Enfield rifles, bayonets, canteens, tents and mess kits. In later years, the curriculum included military history, weapons safety, leadership development, hygiene, land navigation, and psychology of leadership.

At the turn of the twentieth century, participation in military training at Cañon City High School became such a passion to many students – a badge of honor, if you will – that during World War I, Cañon City High School "turned out more men who became officers in the Army than any other school of its size in the country."

Since 1901, Junior Reserve Officer Training Corps (or JROTC) at Cañon City High School has been ongoing and uninterrupted. It continues to thrive during good times and bad, setting the standard for leadership, a sense of family unity, and love of country.

In the 1921 Cañon City High School Annual, the following words were written. To many, they still hold relevance today:

"Military training aims to give each cadet the proper bodily carriage, teaches him the importance of obedience, neatness in personal appearance, concentration of attention and loyalty to home, country, and high ideals. These virtues which are considered of so great importance in the army are certainly expected of all true American citizens."

Local History Center, Cañon City

Cañon City High School Junior ROTC, 1919-1920.

Local History Center, Cañon City

Cañon City High School Rifle Team, 1935-1936.
Front Row, Left to Right - E. Smaller, E. Glass, James Dick, Capt. J.J. Murphy,
Sgt. Hatten, A. Templeton, H. Clark, E. Barnes
Second Row, Left to Right - J. Allen, J. Schultz, Don Bowman, E. Fulkerson,
M. Bergman, C. Watts, Vernon Johnson, Don Donahue

Anderson & Bandholdt
Paint Shop
311 ½ Main Street

During the age of the "resurrectionists," the increase in housing necessitated an increase in the number of those painting those houses. For both professional painters and paint merchants, the two most requested colors were red and white, with red being by far the most utilized simply because it was the least expensive color available. White paint was used sparingly on private homes, with exterior trim, doors, and windows being the obvious recipients of this color. Generally, only secure merchants, bankers or wealthy homeowners would have had the financial means to paint the entire exterior of a dwelling with white paint. To do so was a sign of prosperity; it conveyed a sense of permanence, stability, and respectability.

So it was that Anderson and Bandholdt entered the field of painting in 1882, but for reasons unknown, abruptly ended operations in 1883.

The building that housed the Anderson and Bandholdt Paint Shop was painted red.

Local History Center, Cañon City

Anderson & Bandholdt Paint Shop, 1882.

The St. Cloud Hotel
631 Main Street

In the 1890s, it was the envy of every hotel owner in Colorado. It offered steam heat, electric lights, running water, an elevator, and a first class dining room with linen tablecloths and napkins and snappy waiters. It had thirty guest rooms with private baths (and thirty without) and a horsedrawn carriage to ferry guests from the passenger train depots nearby.

This was the St. Cloud Hotel, one of the finest hotels in Colorado, and long-billed as "The Health Seeker's Resort."

The St. Cloud Hotel was first established not in Cañon City, but in Silver Cliff, Colorado. The year was 1883 and the proprietors were Abell and Bracken. Often mistakenly believed to be the former Powell Hotel, it was built during the apex of the silver mining boom in this historic city. In the early days, if you lived in Cañon City and desired to visit Silver Cliff, you had to take a stagecoach run by the Colorado Stage Express. With a railroad line nowhere near the town, the journey would have taken you seven hours over rough road during unpredictable weather. A railroad did eventually come close to Silver Cliff – about two miles away, in what is now Westcliffe – but when the mining era died, the St. Cloud seemed to die with it. Gone were the miners, the gamblers, dance hall girls, and traveling businessmen who frequented the hotel's well-appointed fifty-five rooms. And gone were the days of reckless abandon when cash flowed easily from barrooms to bedrooms and back again. Most of the ore mills shut down and the population dwindled. The town became a ghost of its former self, so the St. Cloud's owners made the decision that forever changed the future of the hotel: they dismantled it and moved the hotel, brick by brick, to Cañon City.

In the Spring of 1887, the hotel was taken apart, and using freight wagons, hauled to Westcliffe, then loaded onto the Denver & Rio Grande freight cars for the long trip to Cañon City, where the building was reconstructed at its present site at 631 Main Street. At that time, Seventh and Main was considered far from downtown. The city's main business center was located between First and Fourth Streets, with the St. Cloud's primary rival – the McClure House – located on the 400 block. But the St. Cloud's owners had chosen their new location carefully. As the town grew, new residents and new businesses moved eastward – toward the St. Cloud.

When this photograph was taken in 1922
the St. Cloud Hotel was called The Hotel Canon.

Since the relocation of the hotel, Cañon City has seen many changes, and the St. Cloud many owners. The hotel has changed hands almost two dozen times, along with several name changes, as well. During the first twenty-five years of its existence, it was known as the St. Cloud, but when it was sold in 1908, it became the Hotel Denton. The year 1915 brought new ownership and a new name: the Miller Hotel. This was followed by another name change in 1918 to the Hotel Cañon. For sixty-nine years the hotel operated successfully under this name until coming full circle in 1987, with new ownership resurrecting its old name of the St. Cloud Hotel.

In the last one hundred years, the St. Cloud has been the center of many activities, some memorable and positive, others less so. For many years, as early as 1890, it was the site of numerous high school prom celebrations, civic meetings, and Chamber of Commerce banquets. From the 1930s, and lasting many decades, it served as the headquarters of the Continental Trailways office, with buses doing brisk business with departures several times a day. In the 1940s it was the ticket office for Monarch Airlines when it operated out of Fremont County Airport. And yes, in 1927, the north wing of the St. Cloud Hotel also served as state headquarters of the Ku Klux Klan.

Of all the hotels in Colorado, none has been more associated with the entertainment and film industry than the St. Cloud. Buffalo Bill Cody and Calamity Jane stayed here in 1908 when Cody's Wild West Show stopped for a few performances. During the silent picture days of 1910 to 1913, the hotel was the Colorado headquarters for the Selig Polyscope Company from Chicago, and it provided the sleeping quarters for cowboy stars Tom Mix, Bill Duncan, and Joe Ryan. During a huge fire on the fourth floor of the hotel in 1914, the cast and crew of the Colorado Motion Picture Company helped put it out. At the same time, they also gained several hundred feet of footage for a subsequent film project. And from the 1940s on, the building has been home to actors such as Burt Lancaster, Robert Walker, Slim Pickens, Broderick Crawford, Charles Bronson, Scott Brady, Hugh O'Brien, and many others.

In the ensuing years, the fourth floor of the hotel (which was added in 1887 when the three-story building was reconstructed) was converted into six apartments, with the remaining thirty-one guest rooms located throughout the first three floors. Banks, barber shops, coffee houses, beauty shops, gift shops, a men's store, a print shop, dress shops, an art shop and a doctor's office – all have been part of the St. Cloud Hotel's long and colorful history in Cañon City.

Throughout good times and bad, it seems the St. Cloud Hotel has always been a valued and vital member of the community, long in our memories and historically irreplaceable.

Raynolds Bank Building
330-332 Main Street

By the age of twenty-six years, Cañon City's Fred Raynolds became not only the country's youngest bank president, but also Colorado's most dominant banking figure. Raynolds held controlling interest in six banks from Leadville to Buena Vista.

With brothers Joshua and Jefferson, Fred Raynolds opened his first Cañon City bank at the corner quarters of the McClure House in 1874. Before long, the bank moved to the 200 block of Main Street in a building owned by postmaster B. F. Rockafellow. As merchants began moving their businesses east – away from the Territorial Prison – Raynolds followed, setting up his Raynolds Bank building at Fourth and Main.

Completed in 1883, Raynolds Bank – officially the Fremont County Bank – was one of the most impressive buildings in Cañon City at the time, and it remains thus today. Built of coursed ashlar (pink hued stone) from Castle Rock, Colorado, the building's limestone foundation was quarried locally on the grounds of the Territorial Prison, and skilled masons were paid the then-princely sum of $4 per day. The granite columns surrounding the double-door, corner entrance came from Vermont, giving the Gothic Revival architecture a classical and timeless look.

The imposing twenty-foot tower atop the building was removed in 1924, after damage from a devastating storm. It was painstakingly restored in 1982 by local builder Tom Berry, at the behest of owner Wes Carhartt. Using only vintage photographs as models, Mr. Berry spent more than one hundred hours on his incredibly detailed reproduction.

The Raynolds Bank building remained the home of Fremont County Bank (later known as Fremont National Bank) until 1921, at which time Fremont moved to its present location at Sixth and Main.

In 2001 the Raynolds Bank building was restored to its original appearance, and it once again serves as the home of a financial services firm.

Raynolds Bank Building, 1897.

Local History Center, Cañon City

Fremont County Bank Teller Robert S. Lewis
conducting business with patrons (left to right)
Louis Hemmerle and Dana Laurence, 1896.

Local History Center, Cañon City

Fremont County National Bank
at Sixth and Main Streets, 1922.

Circuses, Carnivals, Street Performers, Vaudeville Acts And Parades
331 Main Street

At first glance, this photograph seems to be an unremarkable street scene of downtown Cañon City at 331 Main Street. But the year is 1884, and if you look to the top right-hand portion of this picture – parallel to the third-story of the McClure House – you will see a most improbable sight: an early-day circus tightrope walker.

As long as there has been a Cañon City, there have been circuses, carnivals, street performers, vaudeville acts and parades. The town has never lacked for entertainment of a fantastic nature, nor has it failed to patronize such, commencing with the first real circus to arrive in Cañon City during the summer of 1879, W. W. Cole's New York and New Orleans Circus and Menagerie. The town has also had a very long and rich history of supporting annual community-based events such as Blossom Festivals, Fruit Days, and Flower Carnivals. There have been historic musical and vaudeville performances at the Rex Theatre and Jones Theatre, as well as at the Opera House of so long ago. The pavilion at the hogbacks hosted concerts well into the late 1930s, as did the old bandstand at City Park. Buffalo Bill Cody and Cowboy Tom Mix brought their sold out Wild West shows to College Avenue. The Armory has been the site of dozens of entertainment events since 1927, and the many traveling carnivals of the 1930s to the 1950s set up camp in what is now Veterans Park.

The fellow in the photograph walking the tightrope could have been Dyke Engleman, a Cañon City resident and father of legendary circus performer Bird Millman (Jennadean Engleman). Dyke was an accomplished performer in circuses and vaudeville stages all across North America. He was also the son of M. M. Engleman, a businessman who operated a general store in Cañon City at the time of this photograph.

Tightrope walking was a standard method that circus owners used to drum up business without actually having to expend any revenue. All you needed was a long rope and something to attach it to on both ends – and someone brave enough to walk across it. The McClure House served the attachment purpose well. It was located in the center of town, was the hub of activity, and many performers stayed at the hotel. In no time – with prior notice given to the local newspaper's

A crowd gathers for a performance in front of
the McClure House, 331 Main Street, 1884.

photographer – a crowd would gather for a seemingly impromptu performance, offering just a mere taste of what was to come later under the Big Top.

Vaudeville acts disappeared from Cañon City decades ago. The opera house collapsed from the weight of heavy snow, the bandstand in City Park was razed in the 1930s, and the pavilion at the hogbacks washed away in 1939. Both Buffalo Bill Cody and Tom Mix have gone to that great Wild West show in the sky.

Today more than a century after the town's formation, traveling circuses still come to Cañon City, setting up their tents at the fairgrounds on Elm Avenue. Veterans Park now hosts summer concerts, and lavish parades still march down Main Street.

Newspaper advertisement promoting Buffalo Bill's
Wild West Show in Cañon City on September 4, 1908.

The Mercury
Fifth And Main Streets

Long before *USA Today*, there existed in Cañon City in 1884, *The Mercury*, one of three daily newspapers catering to the news-thirsty populace. Situated in downtown in a brick building surrounded by wood plank sidewalks and a dusty road, *The Mercury* battled *The Cañon City Advance* and the *Rocky Mountain Guide* for subscribers. It was a hard business to be in, as *The Mercury* ended operations by 1885.

In spite of the hardships associated with having to set type by hand, using glue pots and hand-operated presses, and angering many of the local political factions with unpopular editorials, newspapers seemed to be everywhere. Commencing with H. S. Millett's well-written *Cañon City Times* in 1860, Fremont County has seen more than sixty publications come and go in the last almost 150 years, most of which were weekly newspapers. Names such as *The Pioneer*, *The Avalanche*, *Daily Express*, and *Exparte* graced the parlors of most of the city's homes. It was probably no coincidence that the more fierce the competition, the more sensational the news. Very few papers survived more than one or two years.

Today, Cañon City supports the *Cañon City Daily Record* (a daily since 1906, and a weekly since 1885), the *Cañon City Shopper*, the *Canyon Current*, and *Cañon Beat*.

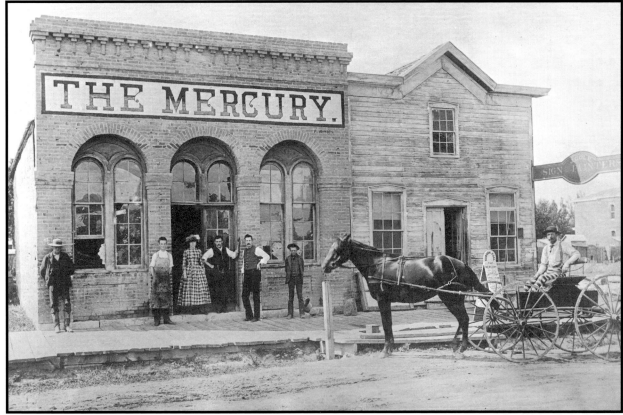

Local History Center, Cañon City

The Mercury, 1884.
To the right of the Mercury building stood J. Cole's Paint Shop
located in a building badly in need of paint.

Cañon City Public Library
516 Macon Avenue

In the early 1880s, Cañon City was a small town with some big ideas. Due primarily to its newfound position as an agricultural paradise, the city was growing rapidly. School districts were formed and buildings constructed to accommodate the hundreds of new students. Businesses of every type were established within city limits. The town had finally become far more than just a way station for stagecoaches and freight lines.

But in spite of the city's commitment to growth, Cañon City did not yet have a public library.

History has long demonstrated and foretold that our best education often comes by way of self-education. To many dreamers and scholars alike, those teachings have commenced at the local free library. Many children have read the adventures of the Hardy Boys, and for a moment, have become the Hardy Boys. These volumes can often take us to other lands and to other lives, and they freely allow us to dream of things that could be. Books speak to us in words and pictures that are both real and imagined. They give us hope for our future, and knowledge for our hearts.

So it was with these thoughts in mind that Mrs. Charles Waldo, Mrs. J. F. Campbell, and Mrs. T. M. Harding, Sr. formed the Cañon City Ladies Library Association in the Spring of 1886. This small group of strong and determined women met in the home of Mrs. Campbell. In quick order they recruited the most prominent and powerful women in this frontier town and developed an ambitious plan for the establishment of the Cañon City Free Library and Reading Room. In several short months, these members, which eventually totaled more than one hundred ladies, formed "baby buggy brigades" that singularly canvassed the entire town from River Street to Rudd Avenue (then being the most northern part of town), soliciting citizens for donations of both cash and books, all of which were carted away in actual buggies. Funds were also raised through bake sales, teas, suppers, and going house to house selling memberships in the association for twenty-five cents per month. It was not long before almost every person in town had become a member of the new library.

Before the month of August of 1886 had ended, the Ladies Library Association had accumulated enough revenue and books for the library. They chose an old, but empty, building at 505 Main Street for the city's first free lending library. Owned by the Denver & Rio Grande Railroad's chief

Ward Collection

Cañon City Public Library, 1905.

engineer, Colonel Greenwood, in a matter of a few weeks, the brick building's trim was painted, wallpaper was hung (for $19), carpet cleaned (for $2), and book shelves and counters built (courtesy of the husbands of the library's ladies).

Cañon City's new library was a resounding success. The building housed not only 2,746 books in 1886, but it also became the home for several display cases filled with fossils, minerals, native stones, and many, many maps of the region.

The building at 505 Main Street served as the library's location for fifteen years, until 1901. With more than five thousand volumes, more space was needed. In a bold move that astounded the community, in 1900 the ladies conveyed the library's entire collection to the city. They changed the institution's name to the Cañon City Public Library, to be governed by a new board of directors, all of whom already were members of the Ladies Library Association.

On December 18, 1901, Mrs. J. M. Ragsdale, president of the Ladies Library Association, received the following letter from the office of philanthropist Andrew Carnegie, responding to the association's request for building funds:

"Mr. Carnegie thinks that Ten Thousand Dollars might cover the cost of a suitable Free Library building for Cañon City... Mr. Carnegie will be glad to provide the above-mentioned sum..."

At the December 1901 meeting of the library association, a building committee was formed. By February of 1902, at a meeting at Elks Hall, the group voted to purchase the two lots where the vacant Presbyterian Church was setting, which was between Fifth and Sixth Streets on Macon Avenue. Wealthy resident Dall DeWeese opposed the purchase of the lots, believing the location to be unsuitable for the library's needs. Ultimately, however, Mayor Peabody (later Governor Peabody) sided with the association and the purchase was made – without further dissent – at a cost of three-thousand five hundred dollars. The church on the site was sold to the Territorial Prison for $140. The inmates later dismantled the building for its lumber.

With the city's blessing, and Carnegie's supporting grant, work began on the new library building. On July 4, 1902 the cornerstone of the fifty-six foot by sixty foot red and white stone building was laid, but by September it was realized that the building fund needed an additional three thousand dollars to complete the project. Once again, Andrew Carnegie agreed to the association's request, and these funds were added to his original bequest.

The Cañon City Public Library was dedicated on January 5, 1903. Since that time, the library's holdings have increased to over sixty-thousand pieces, and the building has been enlarged by five-thousand square feet.

LOCAL HISTORY CENTER

It was on November 27, 1984 that Cañon City's Local History Center was dedicated in a public reception by the mayor of the city. First known as the Colorado History Room, it was located in the basement of the newly expanded library.

In 1986, the Fremont-Custer Historical Society hired long-time resident Cara Fisher to serve as curator of the center, and with a staff of twenty volunteers, worked long hours attempting to survey and catalog the initial collection from the Historical Society.

Far more than simply a repository of old records, the Local History Center is arguably the state's first and most successful model of cooperation between a library and a local historical society in maintaining local history collections. Although collections are added almost daily, Cañon City's Local History Center's holdings include not only rare, historical books and documents, but also scarce city directories, oral history recordings and transcripts, manuscript collections, business journals and ledgers, high school annuals, newspapers, maps, and one of the most impressive vintage photograph collections in the state.

With a dedicated and highly trained and learned staff, in recent years the Local History Center has become the center of research for writers, genealogists, historians, and those seeking information on long lost family histories.

The Local History Center in Cañon City is not only a model for the state, it is the envy of every small town in America.

The Power Plant
U. S. Highway 50

Scarcely seven years after Thomas Edison's invention of the electric light, Cañon City's first commercial electric power plant went into operation. The year was 1886, and the Cañon TH Electric Works Company began producing modest amounts of electricity for primarily town merchants. Believed to be located next to the river bridge on South Ninth Street where the VFW building now stands, no photographs of the plant survive, and the power station ceased operation after two years.

In 1890, Cañon City Electric Light & Power Plant – quickly renamed Colorado Power & Light – began producing electricity for both merchants and town residents alike. Originally located in a small building at 212 South Fifth Street, the plant had the then-impressive capacity to generate electricity at sixty horsepower. But before the year was out, the company's name was again changed to reflect its new venture – ice making – and it became the Cañon City Ice, Light, & Power Company. By 1889, its capacity had increased to one-hundred-sixty horsepower, enough to power 1800 incandescent lights and produce more than ten tons of ice per day.

Through consolidation with other regional power companies, the plant's name was again changed in 1897 to The Colorado Electric Power Company. By then, the company had relocated to its present site at the west end of town, across from the Territorial Prison and the Soda and Mineral Iron Springs. This newly updated facility employed eight workers with a combined annual payroll of $7,200.

Between 1911 and 2002, through sales and continued consolidation, the power plant became known as the Arkansas Valley Railway Light & Power Company (1911), the Southern Colorado Power Company (1923), WestPlains Energy (1990), and Aquila (2002).

The power plant's original home at 212 South Fifth Street later became the site of a Baptist church, a Southern Colorado Power Company warehouse, and the Cañon City Fine Arts Center. It is now the proud home of the *Cañon City Shopper*.

Local History Center, Cañon City

The Power Plant, C. 1940.

State Park At The Territorial Prison
U. S. Highway 50

In an age of land development, expansion and over-building, it is now difficult to believe that the vast open space you see in the accompanying photograph stretched from just below the State Armory on First Street, all the way to the front of the State Prison, almost to the entrance of the power plant.

As early as perhaps 1890, members of the community would regularly walk down to the Soda Springs, just steps from the prison, grab a cold, clear jug of water and stop at State Park on the way back. If it was a Sunday afternoon, then you would have timed your journey to coincide with the weekly concerts given by a handful of inmate musicians from the prison. By the 1920s, the band was so well established that Professor Earle Stowe and his Colorado Prison Band performed at the State Fair in Pueblo, the Royal Gorge Rodeo and rodeo parades, in addition to the weekly concerts in the park.

During the same era, the Cañon City Chamber of Commerce had established a very popular and well-attended zoo within the confines of the park. Their first arrivals were bobcats, eagles and coyotes; then elk and badgers soon followed.

By the 1930s the zoo no longer existed, yet the current warden at the time – Roy Best – proposed adding a playground and turning the park into a gardener's delight by planting twenty-eight different kinds of flowers, in nineteen separate flower beds throughout State Park. In addition, several long unused eagle pens were converted to pheasant cages. By 1935, the flower gardens had become a pleasant reality to the community.

Unfortunately, by 1950, State Park had been fenced off to the public (except for the weekly concerts), the road (Main Street) that led to the prison was rerouted to U. S. Highway 50, and the Soda Springs was destroyed when U. S. Highway 50 was widened.

In 1964, the weekly concerts by the Colorado Prison Band were discontinued.

That vast open space of State Park is now a combination of parking lots, buildings, and U. S. Highway 50.

Local History Center, Cañon City

State Park, Labor Day, September 1, 1918.

Tunnel Drive
The Royal Gorge

In an area filled with so many natural wonders, it seems unreasonable that one area of beauty and curiosity was initially decidedly unnatural. Such is the case of Tunnel Drive.

It was in 1892 that the Kansas-Colorado Irrigation Company was formed to build an irrigation ditch that would carry water from the Arkansas River at the west end of town, to parts east between Cañon City and Pueblo. It was a grand plan to turn those vast plains into lush orchards, hay fields, and vegetable gardens. Again using the very dependable inmate labor from the Territorial Prison, it was called the State Ditch because the project was financed using state funds, and approved by the state legislature. But things did not go exactly as planned.

The State Ditch project called for drawing water from a large wooden pipe set at the edge of the river at the Royal Gorge, snake it via the ditch along the north bank of the gorge through Skyline Drive, to the undeveloped north end of town, then onward to the plains. The inmates started work in 1895, using mostly hand tools and wagons to move and transport many tons of earth and rock. The ditch was to run almost three miles, and the most difficult part of the project entailed digging the three tunnels through the rock at Fremont Peak, and blasting a tunnel through Skyline Drive. The work proceeded very slowly but purposefully – until they reached Skyline Drive.

Situated on the east side of the hogbacks lay the grounds to St. Scholastica Academy and several private homes. When the blasting crew dynamited an opening through Skyline Drive, the resulting tremor was so great that it rocked the foundation of the Academy and several homes, causing extensive damage throughout the area. Lawsuits were threatened and the state legislature became involved. Ultimately, the state settled with the claimants and the project was quietly stopped soon thereafter by Governor James H. Peabody, a resident of Cañon City. It was suggested at the time that the true reason for halting the project was because the state had failed to secure water rights. Whatever the reason for the closure, the State Ditch had thus far cost taxpayers $220,000, with nothing to show for it – save for a few unnatural tunnels.

For years the State Ditch lay unfinished and unused, overgrown with weeds and strewn with rocks and debris. The city eventually took control of the ditch in 1908 and buried a thirty-inch water line that ran the three miles into the gorge area. The city also built iron bridges to carry the water lines in several unsecured spots along the way. The tunnels were enlarged to allow carriages and automobiles to pass through them, and by 1909, this road was being called Tunnel Drive.

Tunnel Drive was a highly visited area by travelers until about 1990, when the old trestle bridges were deemed unsafe and the road was closed. However, through the monumental efforts of Cañon City's Recreation District, the City of Cañon City, local firefighters and the Boy Scouts, along with some new state funding, the old bridges were rebuilt in 2000 and Tunnel Drive reopened to visitors. And to ensure that the area remains a hiker's trail, automobiles are no longer allowed to traverse the entire three mile span of Tunnel Drive.

Finally, an inmate work crew from the Territorial Prison returned to put the finishing touches on a project first began by their predecessors more than one hundred years ago.

Local History Center, Cañon City

Tunnel Drive, C. 1912.

The Cañon City Hose Team of 1893
411 Macon Avenue

Long before fire trucks and horse-drawn fire equipment, and after bucket brigades, came the Cañon City Hose Teams.

Prior to the twentieth century, Cañon City's firefighters were mostly volunteers. The first fire department was the Relief Hook & Ladder Fire Company No. I, established on January 27, 1879. It consisted of one hook and ladder company with an all-volunteer team of twenty-three members. By November of 1880, a second firefighting team was established with the F. A. Raynolds Hose Company No. I, comprised of twenty volunteers.

The hose teams of the 1890s were considered the best-trained firefighters of the nineteenth century. Imagine the supreme physical effort needed by eight to ten men pulling a hundred feet of water hose several city blocks, running as quickly as they could, then having to fight that fire upon arrival. Communities would often send their fastest and most efficient teams to compete in Cañon City's annual Labor Day, Fourth of July and Fruit Day competitions. These teams were, arguably, the best-conditioned firefighting athletes of any era. Dressed in tight-fitting leotard-like outfits, and sporting athletic shoes with spikes, each team would make a mad dash across the dirt streets of several city blocks, pulling the large hose wheel behind them. The goal was to be the fastest from the starting point to the designated hydrant, then the fastest to hook up that hose to the hydrant to get the water to flow. The quickest man on the Cañon City team was also the team's trainer, W. C. West, who regularly ran and won the one-hundred yard dash in about ten seconds. But the real show for most spectators was the impromptu water fight between the hose companies after the competition.

The hose competitions were a source of tremendous pride to the Cañon City community, but often taken a bit too seriously by some, as evidenced by the front page editorial in the *Cañon City Clipper*, admonishing the team in the piece titled, "Getting In Order":

"The Cañon team won in (the) straight-away race, and ran fast enough in the wet test races but fell down in the coupling matter. That feature should receive a great deal of consideration in the present training. The training should be thorough to prevent nervousness and to secure speed and accuracy in making the attachments."

The Cañon City Hose Team, July 1893.

Just before the turn of the century, the fire company added its first paid firemen to its new headquarters at 411 Macon Avenue, as well as maintaining two of the three volunteer hose companies. Three paid firemen earned about sixty dollars per month each. The department also added a two-horse team to pull the heavy wagon laden with hose and ladders. The first horses put into service were named Chief and Taylor. By 1908, the fire house location was again changed when the city built a new station at 211 North Fourth Street.

In 1910, after years of flawless service, Chief and Taylor were retired to pasture and replaced by two large horses named Tom and Dexter. Five years later, these horses were replaced by Cañon City's first motorized equipment, a 1915 Buick touring car that was modified with hose and ladder attachments. The old Buick lasted until 1936 when it was traded in for an actual Seagrave fire truck.

Although the volunteer hose companies of Cañon City were a thing of the past by the 1920s, their speed in firefighting was legendary, and their effectiveness was unmatched - even by today's standards.

Sept. 25 - 1895.

Royal Hubbell Photo

Geo. B. McAulsy Hose Co., No. 1. "Little Giants of Custer."

T. W. Grosser.   W. K. Fellows.   G. C. Dietz.   Ed. Ryon.

John Walts.   F. Folhsm.   W. C. Vorreiter.   W. E. Morley.   E. W. Thomas.

J. A. Smith.   F. X. Miller.   H. J. Brewer.   M. Reddington.

Local History Center, Cañon City

The Cañon City Fire Department in 1912, at 211 N. Fourth Street.
Left to Right: George Padgett, Assistant Captain; Charles McKissick, Sr., Captain;
George Cassidy, Chief; and Fred Priest, Plugman. The horses are Tom and Dexter.

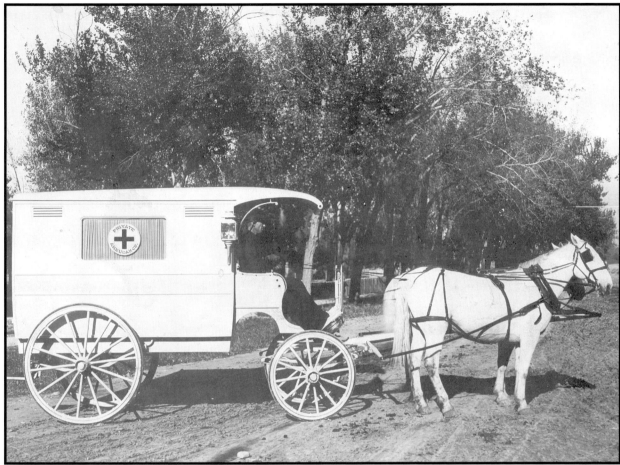

Local History Center, Cañon City

Charles McKissick driving what is believed to be
Cañon City's first ambulance, C. 1910.

S. D. Elliott
Harness & Saddles
507 Main Street

When Sam Elliott left his childhood home of Rising Sun, Indiana to seek his fortune in the West, he arrived in Cañon City on January 1, 1881. Although only twenty-one years of age, he quickly learned the leather business by taking work as he could in livery stables and ranches. For freighters, prospectors, miners, stagecoach owners and local ranchers, the need for a good and dependable leather man was paramount to their survival.

So it was that in 1891, after ten years of laboring for others, Sam Elliott began his own leatherworks business at 507 Main Street. Possessed of a keen mind and uncanny memory, Sam could easily remember the details of a conversation with a customer he had met but once – years prior. The quality of his work was legendary, and he had many repeat customers across the entire state of Colorado. Far more than a workman, he was a true artisan whose work – building and designing saddles, harnesses and bridles – was recognized throughout the region as being the best in the West.

For thirty-five years Sam Elliott was an important and vital member of the community. He had built and sustained lifelong friendships and business relationships with his easy manner and friendly resolve. His small Main Street business continued to thrive even during the madly-popular early years of the horseless carriage.

Yes, for Sam Elliott, life had been good. He had a respected business, a caring and supportive spouse, and five grown children. He knew he was fortunate to have made his place in the world in Cañon City, and the city certainly benefited from his decision to come here in 1881 as a young man with youthful dreams.

Sam Elliott's world came to an abrupt end on the morning of July 20, 1916. After a week-long illness, he died at the age of fifty-six years. A newspaper account at the time mentioned that he had "...lingered between life and death until his vitality was exhausted."

When Sam Elliott died, S. D. Elliott Harness & Saddles died with him. Although difficult to find, a few of Sam's custom-made saddles still survive today, and all are highly valued collector's items.

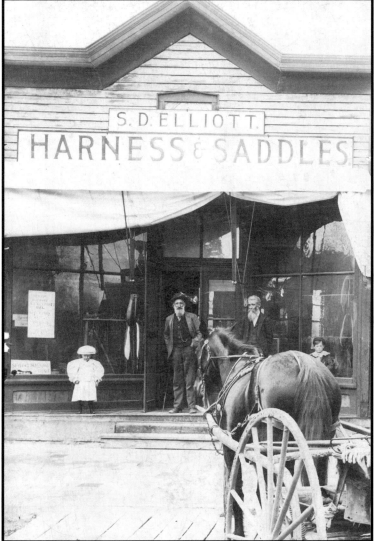

Local History Center, Cañon City

S.D. Elliott Harness & Saddles, 1893.

A. P. Nelson's Grocery
525 Main Street

When this photograph was taken in 1905, Cañon City boasted no fewer than thirteen separate and distinct grocery stores, serving a population half the size of today's inhabitants. Few families had automobiles, and mass transit was nonexistent, so each small section of the community had its own local grocery.

A. P. Nelson's Grocery was originally located at 623 Main Street as early as 1898, but when Guy Hardy built his Record Block building in 1901 at a cost of $10,000, the store's owners moved the grocery into this new 525 Main Street address. The space in the same building at 523 Main Street was used for the offices of Hardy's *Cañon City Record*, which was praised as having the most modern newspaper operations in the state. With its golden oak partitions and furniture, one local merchant described the front office rooms as being "...finer than are found in the swellest city bars or banks."

The Nelson's store was typical of the grocery stores of that era. The proprietors offered primarily dry goods such as fancy coffees and teas, and Monarch brand canned fruits, vegetables and fish. The oversized wicker chairs in the photograph served the dual purpose of offering relief for tired customers, and acted as the store's accounting center. They liked to advertise that they had a "ladies cozy waiting room," and that they also enjoyed a new, fashionable telephone. Their telephone number was prominently displayed as number Red 222, despite the fact that very few of the town's residents could actually afford the luxury of a telephone with which to call them.

Unlike today's one-stop shopping establishments, fresh fruits, vegetables, and dairy and meat products had to be purchased from independent merchants who specialized in these perishable items.

Nelson's Grocery, with five employees and two horse-drawn delivery wagons, operated at this location until its closing in 1908. A. P. Nelson and Clyde Nelson, brothers from MacPherson, Kansas, then opened Nelson's Bakery (also known as Nelson's Caterers) at 609 Main Street. Clyde later became sole owner by acquiring his brother's interest in the shop. He quickly expanded the store's inventory by offering fancy candies and cakes that rivaled William Ott's Candy Company two blocks away. And as the accompanying photograph suggests, those bar stools were meant for patrons of

A. P. Nelson & Co. Grocery Store, 1905.

Nelson's new soda fountain, where customers could enjoy an ice cream soda for a dime, or a whipped cream-topped sundae for fifteen cents.

Seen above the neat rows of candy counters and baked goods is the typically large but slow-moving ceiling fan, surrounded by the numerous big game trophies that were on loan from Dall DeWeese, which are now on display in the Municipal Museum.

By the 1930s, Nelson's Bakery was sold and Clyde Nelson became Cañon City's Chief of Police for several years. The bakery was later known as the Silver Grill.

In ensuing years, this site at 525 Main Street became the home for the Hunter Palmer Drug Store, a Super Drug Store, and Sig's Appliances. By 1968, the *Cañon City Daily Record* had taken over the entire building. But in 1996 the newspaper finally left their long-time home for a new modern facility at 701 South Ninth Street.

Local History Center, Cañon City

Nelson's Caterers, C. 1915.

Ward Hospital
602 Macon Avenue

Cañon City's oldest surviving hospital building was built in 1900 at a cost of six-thousand dollars. Dr. Levi B. Ward built the then-astounding 20 room hospital on heavily-treed Macon Avenue. A graduate of the Kentucky School of Medicine in 1895, he left a promising position at Louisville General Hospital. His goal was to travel to Cañon City in order to set up a practice specializing in the treatment of tuberculosis. So popular was the area for the treatment of such maladies that Ward Hospital became the center for the city's eighteen physicians. Considered modern and innovative for its time, the hospital contained x-ray equipment, a laboratory, an operating room, hot air baths, a delivery room, a nursery, and a kitchen.

It is unfortunate to also note that Dr. Ward did not live long enough to see the full realization of his dream. On February 24, 1903, just three years after the hospital opened, Levi Ward died of pneumonia at the age of 47 years – and as one of the original members of the Elks Club, he was the first member to die. The hospital was immediately closed.

Less than one year later, Ward Hospital was bought by Dr. C. H. Graves. Graves was a long-time railroad physician, and like so many before him, he, too, had come to Cañon City for health reasons. With his son, Dr. Herman Graves, they substantially enlarged the center and renamed it Graves Hospital. Together they practiced until 1936 when the hospital was sold to Drs. D. A. and J. H. Shoun. Soon after the purchase, the center's name was changed to Colorado Hospital.

Commencing in 1950, Dr. Russ Denzler operated the hospital for a short period until selling it to Dr. J. C. Hurliman. Hurliman closed the hospital but continued to practice out of a small office in the building until 1966.

In 1985, Colorado Hospital at 602 Macon Avenue was converted into a sixteen-unit apartment building.

The former Ward Hospital, C. 1940.

St. John's Bicycle Shop
620 Main Street

Spencer Howard St. John relocated from Chicago to Canon City in 1889 for the health of his son, Burt, ill with tuberculosis. Burt died shortly after their arrival, but Spencer decided to remain, as the region's climate was agreeable to his own health.

St. John immediately found work as a machinist in the shop of Hyde & Peabody, but abruptly left to seek his fortune in the gold-laden hills of Cripple Creek. When gold eluded him, he quickly returned to Cañon City, and in 1900, started his own bicycle shop. More than a repairer of bicycles, he built and designed specialty bikes, and was the eventual holder of eleven patents. His inventions ranged from a barbed wire machine to an oil well sand screen. And from his simple shop came perhaps his greatest achievement: the first Colorado-built automobile.

Designed and completely handbuilt in his bicycle shop in 1901, the St. Johnmobile was a two-bench seater that could comfortably carry four adults. At two-and-a-half horsepower, the vehicle could speed along at a steady 12 mph, and once traveled to Pueblo from Cañon City in a little over three hours. St. John also started an automobile repair shop, but it appears he never seriously pursued the mass marketing of his vehicles.

Spencer St. John lived to be ninety-one years old. He was still active in his little machine shop until just a few months before his death in 1938.

Local History Center, Cañon City

St. John's Bicycle Shop, 1901.

The Elks Lodge Building
404 Macon Avenue

It was on July 30, 1900 that a small group of gentlemen from Cañon City gathered together to institute Lodge 610, The Benevolent and Protective Order of Elks. These were not just ordinary men, but the most powerful, wealthy and influential men that the city had to offer. The membership list over the next several years was a virtual Who's Who of pioneers and business leaders, with names such as Maupin, Rockafellow, Little, Trout, Hardy, Ward, Dozier, Higgins and Hemmerle.

Nationally, the Order of Elks was originated on February 16, 1868 by a group of fifteen actors and other theater people who called themselves The Jolly Corks. The leader of the group, Charles Vivian, referenced himself as the Imperial Cork. Initially they had gathered for social reasons, but later decided to become a fraternal group to contribute to charitable causes. A new name was obviously needed. The name of Elk was selected because this large animal was "distinguished by its fleetness of foot and was timorous of wrongdoing."

Benevolence did become the true focus of this early group, as it continues to be today. With more than two-thousand chapters and well over one-million members, the Elks have raised and contributed untold millions for civic and charitable causes nationwide.

Elks Lodge 610 first met at Shaeffer Hall, located at 426-428 Macon Street in 1900. Some weeks later they moved to the second floor of the F. L. Smith building at Fifth and Main Streets.

From the original charter membership of forty-five men, by 1911 the list had grown to almost five-hundred members, far too many to comfortably fit into the Smith building. As early as 1907, plans were underway to find a new Elks Hall, with a building committee being selected in 1909.

Finally, property at Fourth and Macon Streets was purchased from Morton S. Bailey for $6,500. And by May of 1911, plans for the Classical Revival-styled building had been approved and a contractor chosen with the low bid of $26,242.

Elks Hall was opened for a public viewing and reception on February 8, 1912, with a formal dedication on February 22nd. The meal served at the dedication, donated by cattlemen from Fremont, Custer and Park Counties, consisted of barbecued elk.

The Elks Lodge, 1920.

Brother Elks out for a spin in Charles Pauls' 1904 Cadillac.
Pictured are (from left to right): Dentist G. H. Kellenberger, D. Lindenberg,
Dan Garret, Charles Pauls (drinking), Bing Towler (with can in hand),
Henry Beckham, and Judge Kent Eldred.

Payton's Millinery And
Ladies Furnishings Store
522 Main Street

It was March 15, 1901 – about the same day this photograph was taken – that Emma Payton opened her parlor that catered to the fashion needs of Cañon City's ladies. Her specialization was in the sale of hats, evidenced by the large number of such in the cases to the right, and lined-up atop the counters, all the way to the back of the store.

By the end of the nineteenth century – and well into the twentieth century – ladies' hats were probably the most popular form of personal adornment available to most women. Hats with silk ribbons, fresh flowers and feathers of various shapes and sizes became all the rage. There were tall hats and short hats, wide hats and narrow hats. Hats from San Francisco, New York, Paris and London set the standards for all hats everywhere. There were hats for every occasion and every purpose. There were hats with veils for the "come hither" look. There were practical hats for shopping, and dark hats for funerals. There were summer hats for special outings or celebrations. And to the collective befuddlement of all men everywhere, there seemed to be new hats every Easter.

Incredible hats were everywhere, and they were beautiful.

Although hats were the dominant items in her store, they were not Mrs. Payton's only products. Notice the elegant dresses, petticoats and boxes of notions throughout the store. There is little doubt she also carried those unspeakable items (underthings) mysteriously hidden away somewhere in the darker recesses of the store.

Described as a person of culture and skill, Emma Payton employed as many as eight assistants in her quaint little shop. By all accounts, the store was managed successfully and profitably.

However, for reasons unknown, Mrs. Payton's "Emporium of Fashion" was no longer doing business in Cañon City after 1902.

Local History Center, Cañon City

Payton's Millinery, 1901.

The Ceylon Tea Store
521 Main Street

Exuding an atmosphere of sophistication commensurate with the "higher class" of clientele that the city's founding fathers had long sought as residents, the Ceylon Tea Store was a very uncommon business in a very unlikely setting, with a completely unexpectedly long business life.

Established in 1900 at 714½ Main Street, the store was first named Coolbaugh's Tea Store. But by May of 1901, proprietor Robert S. Coolbaugh had changed both the store's location and its name – and he had a new angle. Coolbaugh believed that the name "Ceylon" would evoke a more-worldly perspective to his establishment. While coffee shops had come and gone, no one had yet attempted to showcase a simple tea shop in Cañon City using an Asian theme, run by a native Midwesterner. There would be no cowpokes stopping by after a long cattle drive, to be sure; but with the shop's fine china, delicate wall fixtures and fan back chairs, it did appeal to those of more refined tastes.

The Ceylon Tea Store offered freshly-ground fine coffees, exotic spices from both the Far East and Middle East, extracts and a large variety of mixed teas. At the store, Coolbaugh sold hot teas, brewed teas, organic teas, and health teas, all of which he was able to blend on the premises. But, oddly, while he promoted the name "Ceylon" (Sri Lanka today), the store's furnishings and decorations all seemed to be of Japanese origin. Even the large parasol that hung from the ceiling was Japanese in design, as were the smaller parasols at the rear of the store.

By 1906, Robert Coolbaugh had decided to move on and the store was sold to his assistant, Charles Duncan, and friend E.C. Wills. In 1910 Duncan acquired Will's interest.

Charles Duncan now owned the store, but its aromatic coffees and teas still flowed from its pots. While he expanded the stock, he continued to feature Coolbaugh's original line of products that had made the shop so different. But he also added a service that made his products more accessible to all residents – home delivery.

With his horse and wagon, Fred Halsted would make house-to-house calls to all of Cañon City's home addresses one day, then deliver the ordered items the following day. As the popularity of home delivery spread, the route expanded to include the coal camps and Lincoln Park. Charles' son, Donald Duncan, later took over the sales route, eventually graduating to a small truck when the shop moved in 1918 to 517 Main Street.

The Duncans continued to operate the tea store until 1943, when it was sold to Mrs. Guy James. Two years later Mrs. James sold out to Robert and Fern Manley. The Manleys retained the store's original charm, but added women's clothing, pottery and crystal to their stock. During the Christmas holidays they also sold hundreds of locally-made fruitcakes.

In 1955, Mr. And Mrs. Cecil Snyder bought the Ceylon Tea Store from the Manley family. They managed the store for two years, then closed it down and moved to Florence, ending the final chapter of this incredible and unique downtown Cañon City business.

Ceylon Tea Store, Robert S. Coolbaugh, Proprietor, 1903.

Cañon City:
The Motion Picture Capital Of The West
314 Main Street

At first glance, the title above seems a little improbable, given the countless number of Western films made in this country in the last one hundred years. But the title is a valid one; in fact, Cañon City might well have been the motion picture capital of the entire country during the silent film era from 1902 to 1914.

During the first few years of the twentieth century, the major film studios were located in New York, New Jersey, Philadelphia, and Chicago. As audiences became more sophisticated, they began demanding more realistic settings. Cardboard backgrounds were acceptable for interior scenes and parlor settings, but Jersey landscapes were poor substitutes for Ponderosa pines and dusty trails. To accommodate these viewers, location shootings were staged in Florida and Missouri; then in Oklahoma, Arizona, and finally, Colorado.

The Selig Polyscope Company of Chicago was the first major studio to commit resources and labor to Cañon City. Their first movies filmed in Colorado were very short, two-minute travelogues of the Rockafellow orchards and neighboring mining areas. But as they began to understand the potential of Cañon City as a Western setting for cowboy pictures, the films increased in length to fifteen-minute one-reelers. These films were often violent, vigilante films, where the storyline dictated that the villain would always get his deadly comeuppance. They were followed by two-reel feature films, which were shot in two or three days. Film stock was very costly and budgets quite sparse, so actors were expected to hit their mark quickly, on cue, and then move on. "One-takes" were the norm, and reliable actors such as William Duncan, Josephine West, Myrtle Stedman, and the father of all Western film stars, Gilbert Anderson, found steady work in Colorado. Anderson, later known as Bronco Billy Anderson, filmed many of his more than three hundred Western films in Colorado, and some even in Cañon City.

It is a convincing argument that the two individuals most responsible for bringing filmmaking to Cañon City were Otis B. Thayer, a director for Selig Polyscope, and unknown actor Tom Mix. Thayer had visited Cañon City as an actor. He had performed at the opera house years prior to his film days. Tom Mix and his wife, Olive, started out as trick riders for the Selig Company in Cañon City

The Colorado Motion Picture Company at Third and Main Streets,
with director and producer Otis B. Thayer
standing on the vehicle's running board, 1913.

in 1911. At the same time, he was also working as the night marshall in San Animas, and later as a ranch hand for Harding Brothers in Cañon City.

Tom Mix was a publicist's dream. He was an authentic cowboy who had good looks, a steady hand, and a flamboyant on-screen presence – and it did not hurt that he was also the 1909 Royal Gorge Rodeo Champion. Mix would later state that the only reason he entered film acting was to raise enough money to finance his dream of starting his own Wild West Show. At $100 per week from Selig, he was well on his way.

With an office at 314 Main Street that doubled as a stage for interior shots, the Selig Company filmed most of their outdoor scenes at Skyline Drive, Prospect Heights, the Hot Springs Hotel, and in the Garden Park area. Many scenes were also filmed at Hell's Half Acre, a settlement that was home to many of Cañon's saloons – and the source of many of Tom Mix's legendary exploits off screen. One such story repeated by local rancher Woody Higgins is that after a long day of filming, he and Mix would often take turns shooting lemons off the tops of glasses at the Colorado Saloon. The first to miss bought a round of drinks for the house. Tom Mix was also known to "entertain" at the local Elks Club and the McClure Hotel.

Selig Polyscope made eight films in Cañon City in 1911, and another twenty-five in 1912. It was expected that Selig would return the following year to work on an even greater number of films, and as late as January of 1913, all indications pointed in that direction. However, by February the company had packed up and headed for the comfortable year-round weather of Hollywood, which was still primarily orange groves and fruit farms.

One person who did not leave Cañon City was Otis B. Thayer. Under his direction, the Colorado Motion Picture Company was born. The company's first film was "The Hand of the Law", which was filmed at the Territorial Prison. This 1913 film was an unheard of three-reeler. Encouraged by this production, Thayer offered to make Cañon City the studio's permanent home if the city would purchase five-thousand dollars of the company's stock. The city quickly agreed, and by January of 1914, the Colorado Motion Picture Company had established permanent quarters in downtown Cañon City. Warner Features (later to become Warner Brothers) became its distributor, and by the end of August, the studio had completed no fewer than five feature films.

In the early days, filmmaking was serious business and actors were often hurt, disabled, and even killed during production. Horses tripped, wagons tipped, and bulls bucked. The Colorado Motion Picture Company was not immune to such calamities. With seeming disregard for the safety

Ward Collection

Tom Mix as he appeared in 1911.

The Great K & A Train Robbery, 1926.

of the cast and crew, injuries were a frequent occurance. No one was exempt from such injuries, as the company was soon to learn.

On the morning of July 1, 1914, in preparation for a scene in the film "Across The Border", actress Grace McHugh's horse stumbled as they crossed the Arkansas River at the Royal Gorge. She was thrown from the saddle and swept downstream by the fast current. Cameraman Owen Carter jumped in to save her, but he, too, was swept away. Both lost their lives.

Owen Carter's body was found one week later, a mile downstream. Grace McHugh's remains were found thirteen days later by rancher T.R. Williams, two miles below Florence. She was buried in Denver.

The death of Grace McHugh also marked the end of the Colorado Motion Picture Company. The studio went out of business almost immediately, and the era of quickly produced silent Western films in Cañon City died with them.

Tom Mix did eventually make it back to Cañon City for one last visit before he died. He came out of retirement to make the 1935 serial, "The Miracle Rider". The salary that he earned from this film helped finance his lifelong dream – The Tom Mix Wild West & Circus Combined. The circus made its way to Cañon City in 1936, with Tom Mix proudly leading a grand procession of horses and riders down Fourth Street. Local resident and retired school principal Ivan Millhollin remembers that day quite vividly. To six-year-old Ivan, Tom Mix was everything every young boy wanted to be. He recalls that Mix had a broken leg, so he rode on the front fender of his roadster to the fairgrounds. Following along, Ivan watched as the elephants erected the big top, and young Ivan even lent a hand carrying buckets of ice water, which resulted in receiving a snow cone for his help.

Four years later, Tom Mix was dead. On October 11, 1940, after staying the night at the Santa Rita Hotel in Tucson, Arizona, Mix had a short chat in the hotel's parking lot with policeman Dick Lease. His last words to Lease were "So Long". Tom Mix then drove his 1937 Cord 812 Roadster out of town at a high rate of speed to a meeting with fellow cowboy star Ken Maynard. It was only a few minutes later that a passing motorist found the car in a ditch with Tom Mix dead inside. He had failed to negotiate a sudden turn in the road, traveling in excess of 100 mph.

Years passed, and while the number of films shot in Cañon City decreased, it seems the quality of such actually increased. Lee Marvin's "Cat Ballou", John Wayne's "The Cowboys" and his Oscar-winning "True Grit" – all were filmed in Cañon City; as was the Tom Selleck and Sam Elliott epic "The Sacketts", "How the West Was Won" with James Arness, and 1977's "Comes a Horseman".

Ward Collection

1935 Lobby Poster.

Ward Collection

Tom Mix, 1930.

Ward Collection

Tom Selleck and Sam Elliott filmed
"The Sacketts" in Cañon City in 1978.

For those who love Western films, Cañon City has always been – and will always be – hallowed ground worthy of the reverence that early Native Americans bestowed upon the region long before we understood its true importance.

Ward Collection

Gilbert "Bronco Billy" Anderson, the original Western film star, C. 1910.

The Owl Cigar Store
626 Main Street

At the turn of the twentieth century, the popularity of cigars had long overtaken the sales of cigarettes. Both the aristocratic gentleman and the common man could be seen enjoying a long stogie. In fact, it was considered a very proper social statement to be photographed with a cigar in hand, or to have one protruding from a coat pocket. The appearance of such conveyed an air of sophistication, success, and calm resolve. The Cañon City man – from rancher to banker – was no different. The town's growing population quickly and earnestly attempted to leave its Wild West image behind by appealing to those of a more cosmopolitan nature, which brought upscale hotels, an opera house, movie theatres – and yes, even a top-notch cigar shop.

When Fred Sartoris proudly opened his cigar store at the corner of Sixth and Main Streets in 1902, he named his business after his favorite brand, the Owl Cigar. His shop carried every brand of cigar available to the public, including the popular cigars from the Carolinas and Virginia, in addition to the more expensive imported items, which were previously available locally only in the Denver area. And similar to other merchants in town, his store also doubled as a lunch counter. There is little doubt that Fred Sartoris believed that a fine cigar was best appreciated after a fine meal.

By the following year of 1903, and until 1907, The Owl relocated to 628 Main Street; then to 630 Main Street in 1908. By 1929, the store was sold to Fred Luthi and George Bell, who moved the business to its present location at 626 Main Street in 1937,

When James Santilli and son Elmer bought the Owl Cigar Store from Fred Luthi in 1943, the store had already been in business over forty years. But the Santilli family began their own dynasty that year that continues to this day. The Owl is one of the longest continuously running businesses in Cañon City history.

James Santilli passed away in 1945. His three sons, Pete, Elmer and James took over the shop the same year. By 1947, they had expanded the length of the store to accomodate a few good pool tables and patron restrooms, and they also began selling fishing supplies and sports items. But because of the decline in tobacco sales, fewer and fewer cigars were being sold. The store now concentrated on the sale of their now-legendary hamburgers (of which they have sold over one million) and milkshakes.

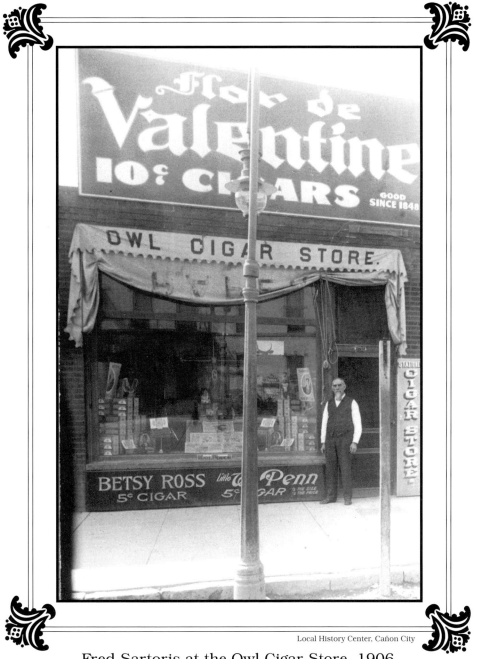

Fred Sartoris at the Owl Cigar Store, 1906.

The Owl Cigar Store has changed very little over the years. It still has its tiled floor, vintage lunch counter and bar stools, fishing trophies, pool tables, and the friendly family atmosphere of long ago. Memorabilia of family and friends, past and present, now grace the walls of the revered downtown establishment.

You can still buy a pretty good cigar there, too.

The Maupin Building
Fifth And Macon Streets

General Joseph H. Maupin was not a general in the military sense. Maupin was a former Colorado state attorney general who served from 1890 to 1892. At thirty-six years of age, he was the youngest person to be elected to that position, and the first Democrat in that post. He was so well liked by his constituents that the title of "general" was one that stuck with him long after his stint in public service. Locally, he was referred to as the "Tall Cottonwood of the Arkansas," or "Honest Joe" during his days as the mayor of Cañon City in 1888.

Joseph Maupin's skills as an attorney and orator were said to resemble those of Abraham Lincoln, as did his tall, thin frame. Similar to Lincoln, his court presence was commanding and his arguments convincing. A former staff member was once quoted as saying that Maupin was thought to have the ability to "… convince the jury that black was white and vice versa."

After his days in law were finished, Maupin built several downtown structures, but the building that bears his name remains his most memorable project.

Between the years of 1903 and 1907, from the porch of his modest cottage in what is now the Cañon City Public Library Park, Joseph Maupin oversaw the construction of a large brick building that immediately served as Cañon City's new post office. On ground that originally held the Christ Episcopal Church, this 17,500 square-foot building, which was designed by architect George Roe of Pueblo, was painstakingly built with four layers of cream-colored brick. The second floor had intricately woven medallions fashioned above the windows, and the first floor windows were large and similarly shaped on the Macon Street side of the building. The large lobby had tile floors and wainscoting, and the second floor hallway was – and remains – seven feet wide, and ten feet high. And since 1907, atop this remarkable building, at the corner entrance, are the words "Post Office Block," and "Maupin." When it was completed, newspaper reports declared the building to be "the finest, most complete and up-to-date post office in the state of Colorado."

Joseph Maupin died in 1926, and by 1929, the Cañon City Post Office had begun construction of a new post office building across the street.

The Post Office officially vacated the Maupin building in 1931. Over the years, the Maupin building has been utilized as law and business offices, a bank and finally, apartments. In 1997, at

The Post Office Block Building -
also known as the Maupin Building, 1908.

a cost estimated at around $100,000, owners Becky and Bill Lowe faithfully and lovingly restored one of Cañon City's most treasured buildings. Today, still referred to as either the Maupin Block Building, or the Post Office Building, the structure now serves as space for twelve upscale apartments and several high profile storefront businesses.

Local History Center, Cañon City

Joseph and Lilly Maupin at
502 Macon Avenue, C. 1900.

Skyline Drive
U. S. Highway 50

Rising eight hundred feet above Cañon City, since 1906 Skyline Drive has offered thousands of visitors a breathtaking view of the city that only early settlers, prospectors and Native Americans had known.

The true origin of the idea for building Skyline Drive is not known. One story holds that D. E. Gibson hitched a team of horses to a handmade plow and attempted (unsuccessfully) to pave such a road himself. Another story that circulated for years promoted the thought that Colonel Frederick E. Greydene-Smith first suggested the road. Still other reports hold that the idea was first dreamed up by various citizens as early as the 1860s. Despite the general lack of clear history in this regard, what is accepted is that the project was started in 1905 at the Fifth Street entrance. State Senator Moses E. Lewis of Florence is credited with clearing the way for the road's construction by getting the Senate to pass his Convict Labor Road law, which provided free inmate labor for public roads projects.

In October of 1905, sixty inmates from the Territorial Prison were given the option of having ten days deducted from their sentence in exchange for every month they worked on the road. Local citizens raised more than $2,000 for tools and blasting powder, and by February the road was nearly completed. The *Cañon City Record* reported on February 12, 1906 that the scenic drive had achieved instant success: "Skyline Drive is about the most popular thing that ever happened. Sunday more than 200 vehicles and probably more than 1,000 people viewed the beauties of this rich valley…"

The mountain range that carries Skyline Drive has always locally been referred to as the hogback. A geologic term, it means an up-tilted rock layer. As the road was being built on the town side of the ridge, a citizens' committee was formed to consider a formal name for this "pleasure driveway," as it was being called. No one was enamored with the suggested names of Hogback Highway, or Hogback Heaven. Other names suggested were Columbia Heights, Alta Vista Boulevard, Grey Cliff Road, Long View Road, and Cliff Drive. But before a final vote could be taken on an agreed-upon name, S. A. Van Buskirk ended the speculation by stating that he had the name "Skyline Boulevard" incorporated in the deed for the land. However, before 1907 was completed, locals began substituting the word "Drive" for the word "Boulevard," and it has remained thus.

Ward Collection

Skyline Drive, 1912.

For a brief period after the road's completion, the hogback was informally called Mt. Cleghorn, in honor of Warden John Cleghorn who provided the inmate labor. And at Van Buskirk's insistence, there was even a fancy stone marker that read, "Cleghorn Scenic Drive – 1906." Neither name stuck, and before long the world embraced the name of Skyline Drive.

It was not long after Skyline Drive opened in the spring of 1906 that conflicts arose between riders of horseless carriages, and those who used horses and buggies. The automobiles – known back then as "buzz wagons" – would often spook horses on this narrow stretch, causing many a tense moment. The city council resolved the issue – temporarily – by banning automobiles from the hogback. Fines of up to fifty dollars and/or ten days in jail were imposed for violators. But the city ordinance did not last very long. By 1907, automobiles were allowed back on the hogback, but only on Tuesday mornings and Friday afternoons. In time, as the automobile overtook the horse and buggy in popularity, the ordinance was eliminated altogether.

Cañon City's entrepreneurial spirit was also very much alive as several businesses were set up to serve the needs of visitors to Skyline Drive. Bill Garton operated a "Tally Ho" tour service, using fourteen teams of horses to haul tourists up and down the scenic highway for 25 cents. Allen Bowen leased a snack shop in a little stone pavilion at the top of Skyline Drive, with the city providing the electricity. But perhaps the most ambitious undertaking was the city's 1934 construction of a fourteen-hundred seat amphitheater between the hogback and the smaller "pigbacks" on the town side of the mountain. On land donated by the Jewett Fire Brick Company, and again using inmate labor, workers using picks and shovels dug out a two-hundred foot area that was named Skyline Bowl. The amphitheater was dedicated on June 12, 1934 with a performance by opera singer Karl Jorn. There were over seven hundred people in attendance, but, sadly, the Skyline Bowl was washed away in a violent storm just a few years later, never to be rebuilt.

One structure that has withstood the test of time is the Skyline Drive Archway, located at the west entrance, just off Highway 50. Financed by the city, but coordinated by the Chamber of Commerce, this impressive archway was built in 1932 using a native stone from every state in the union. It was initially proposed that the archway be built of logs, but the city council desired a more permanent structure. The final design was determined by a committee comprised of service clubs, the city council, and the Chamber of Commerce.

Ward Collection

The entrance to Skyline Drive, C. 1940.

Ward Collection

Skyline Drive, 1919.

The Tally Ho Tour Company escorting sightseers
up Skyline Drive, C. 1910.

Ritzman Cement Works Company
500 South Ninth Street

When Lorentz Ritzman migrated west to Cañon City from Buffalo, New York in 1906, it was not in his plans to be the area's patron saint of cement.

Born in Switzerland in 1862, and trained as a jeweler, at the young age of eighteen years, Lorentz relocated to Jamestown, New York to learn the trade of blacksmithing. After a short visit, he decided that blacksmithing was not to be his chosen profession. After stays in both Pittsburgh, Pennsylvania and Buffalo, New York, where he learned the cement-making business, he and his wife, Emma, journeyed to Cañon City to enter the fast-growing field of fruit-growing in Lincoln Park. At the urging of his brother, Josh, who had moved here years earlier for health concerns, within the span of one year, Lorentz tried his hand at blacksmithing, fruit-farming, and real estate sales. None gave him the satisfaction he sought.

The Ritzman brothers soon observed that there was a dire need for concrete products in Cañon City, so the following year of 1907, the Ritzman Cement Works Company was created. Although the business did not officially start producing cement products until that year, the brothers began construction of their signature building at the end of 1906, and the structure was completed just before the dawn of the new year. With the knowledge that Lorentz had gathered during his time in Pittsburgh and Buffalo, they quickly began producing items of every shape and form imaginable, from concrete pipes to fence posts. In short order, the company became the largest and most prolific provider of concrete products in the Upper Arkansas Valley.

Apparently not wasting any time, the Ritzman brothers also foresaw the need for a hotel on the south side of Ninth Street, not far from the plant. It was still 1907, and by using their own patented stone, they hastily built the Rio Grande Hotel.

Local History Center, Cañon City

Ritzman Concrete Products, 1920.

The Rio Grande Hotel
302 South Ninth Street

The Ninth Street Denver & Rio Grande Railroad Depot was just a short walk from the hotel, which was strategically located at 302 South Ninth Street. Thousands of travelers took comfort in the hotel's eighteen guest rooms – and two baths – in its forty years of operation. The Ritzman brothers owned the building just one year before it was sold. Ownership of the hotel changed hands several times until it was purchased by William F. Ott in 1930. But before that time, the cement plant's name had changed to Ritzman Concrete Products.

Sadly, in 1924, at the height of the Ritzman company's success, Lorentz Ritzman died from injuries sustained when his Ford truck was hit broadside by an east-bound Denver and Rio Grande Western freight train. The accident occurred at the Ninth Street railroad crossing, not far from the cement plant.

Ritzman Concrete Products discontinued operation in the 1960s, after more than fifty years of service to the community that included providing blocks for more than one hundred of the city's homes, and creating many of the town's first concrete sidewalks.

When William Ott purchased the Rio Grande Hotel in 1930, he changed its name to the Ott Hotel. This extremely well built Gothic Revival styled building served as a hotel until about 1947, when the downstairs portion was used by several different merchants. The upstairs portion was unused until the entire building was carefully remodeled and restored in 1995 and 1996 by real estate professional and owner Carolyn Reeves.

Local History Center, Cañon City

The Rio Grande Hotel, 1910.

The Ott Candy Company
418 Main Street

One of the purest pleasures in life is the effect that candy has on our senses, and on our general sense of well-being. The taste, texture and warmth of freshly made chocolate and hard candy puts us in a state of complete and helpless ecstasy for which there seems to be no recovery. Grown men and small children alike have fallen victim to its unrelenting lure, and for a brief moment, life's problems are forgotten, and we are grateful.

William F. Ott's candy store on Main Street was one of the most successful and popular businesses in all of southern Colorado. Founded in 1910, the small, prosperous company would later serve to establish Ott as one of Cañon City's most financially secure and respected citizens.

It was in New York City that he was born in 1870. After a short stay the Ott family of five boys and two girls relocated to Missouri, where William eventually learned the jewelry-making business. For several months in 1890 he practiced his new trade in his own store in Tulsa, Oklahoma, but after its closure, he sold jewelry for the J. R. Woodenson Jewelry Company as a traveling salesman. It was on one such journey in 1900 that he made a stop in Cañon City. It would be a visit that profoundly changed his life.

With a case filled with real and imagined jewels, William went door to door selling his wares to the town's residents. He found the climate agreeable and the people friendly, and tiring of travel, he simply chose to stay. Opening his own jewelry business at a small storefront at the 500 block of Main Street, he made a modest but unremarkable living. Although the town was growing, his business was not growing with it. After ten frustrating years, it became abundantly clear that cowpokes and fruitgrowers were generally not jewelry buyers, so he closed the shop one day and reopened it the next day as The Ott Candy Company.

It must have been quite an unusual sight for the locals when William Ott changed professions in such an abrupt manner. At first, business was slow, but when he changed locations to the 400 block of Main Street, his world changed.

The Ott Candy Company was unlike anything Cañon City had ever seen. William transformed the back room of the store as a bakery, and with a combination of sugar, honey, chocolate and syrup, he prepared many varieties of coated sliced fruit, preserves, bonbons and stick candies. During warm summer days, he would switch on the ceiling fans, effectively pushing the sweet scent of his

Anna Moorefield and Artie Volk,
employees of the Ott Candy Company, 1925.

fresh confections down the street to unsuspecting would-be patrons. As the display cases in the accompanying photograph attest, his store was well-stocked and flowing to the brim with delicacies that residents previously had to have imported from Denver or Colorado Springs.

The candy shop, with its ornate metal ceiling and trim, was a popular novelty frequently visited by both residents and tourists. However, the Palace Drug Store and other local shops began to add soda, malt, and ice cream counters to their establishments, and ever the entrepreneur, so did William.

In 1922, the Ott Candy Company informally became locally known as "Ott's Ice Cream and Candy Shop." The ice cream counter was not just a standard pre-formed item; it was a custom-made twenty-two foot long work of art made of milk glass, framed in a stunningly vivid and polished black marble. The eighteen-foot mirror behind the counter was framed in both marble and handcarved mahogany; the eleven counter steel stools were covered with bright white porcelain, and the seats were made of stained oak. The shop also had a new Hamilton Beach milkshake mixer, along with nickel-plated soda dispensers. Obviously, the theme was white, from the front door to the employee aprons.

The candy and ice cream shop did so well that William Ott was able to buy the Rio Grande Hotel on Ninth Street (next to the railroad tracks) in 1930, and eventually became a major property owner in Cañon City. Often described as a friendly and helpful merchant and friend, almost all of William's financial endeavors flourished until his death in 1941 at seventy-one years of age.

But the story of the ice cream counter did not end with the death of William Ott.

The Ott Candy Company continued to thrive until 1952 when the Ott family sold the shop's beautiful marble and milk glass counter and all equipment to Don Tyner. Mr. Tyner was the original owner of the Royal Gorge Scenic Railroad. He dismantled the ice cream shop's contents, then installed them in a building at the site of the Scenic Railroad. The ice cream shop was a popular addition there until 1983, when the equipment was put into storage. In 1985 the equipment was purchased by Monroe's Gift Shoppe. It was carefully reassembled as William Ott had displayed it, and once again, it became the focal point of the community by becoming the centerpiece of a new shop known as "The Ice Cream Social."

The lobby of the Ott Hotel, C. 1930.
(Formerly the Rio Grande Hotel)

Priest Canyon Road
The Royal Gorge

In an area long closed to the public lay the remnants of a road that commenced just north of the entrance to Skyline Drive, and through twists, turns and switchbacks, proceeded to the top of the Royal Gorge to a spot known as Vista Point.

For years prior to 1900, residents of Cañon City could only dream of a road to Vista Point. After several disappointing attempts to construct such a thoroughfare – one of which included an elaborate electric railroad – a deal was struck between the city and the warden of the Territorial Prison. Judging from the efficient manner in which an inmate crew had constructed Skyline Drive in 1906, it was agreed that a similar crew would build Priest Canyon Road. So in February of 1910, seventy-five inmates equipped with supplies and tools furnished by the city began work on this five mile stretch of highway that ended just east of Buckskin Joe, where the present gorge road is located.

Priest Canyon did not acquire its name from any theological beginnings. Contrary to popular opinion, the canyon's name was simply a tribute given to early settler Jim Priest who had a large ranch at the mouth of the canyon. Described in 1911 by colorful local drugstore clerk H. N. Beecher as "the boulevard of dreams," and a place where "snakes have a kind of Christian Science smile on their faces," Priest Canyon became one of the most visited natural sites in the region after the road was completed that same year. With more than two-thousand people in attendance, this historic road was dedicated on May 12, 1911 by Governor John Shaford, who predicted that the Royal Gorge would become the nation's playground. The event was billed as The Great Gala Royal Gorge Opening. The following day, May 13th, the town celebrated a different event: The Great May Day Flower Carnival, complete with May pole dances, a parade, and a performance by the marching Pueblo Cowboy Band.

Many of the first automobiles to drive up Priest Canyon Road were Model-T Fords. With the road being very steep in places, these early cars often lacked the horsepower to traverse the rough terrain in forward gears, so it became a frequent pastime to journey the highway in reverse, where power was more plentiful. This action was dangerous, foolish, and precarious but thousands attempted it – until their radiators boiled over. To assist travelers in such predicaments, the Cañon City Auto Club opened two natural springs along the trail so that motorists could replenish their vehicles' water supplies. Those who dared travel the road without stopping for water – or carrying extra

Ward Collection

Priest Canyon Road, C. 1912.

water with them – soon found that Priest Canyon Road could also be a very long walk back to town. It was a stroll often fraught with uncomfortable face to face meetings with bears, mountain lions, and rattlesnakes (smiling and otherwise).

The Sangre de Cristo Mountains, Cooper Mountain, Pike's Peak, and the hills of Cripple Creek – all could be seen from atop Vista Point, one of the most majestic settings in all of Colorado. So it was for this reason that in 1921 two free-thinking ladies from California – Cora Beardsley and Ethel McMullin – chose this area for their restaurant, lodge, dance hall and tourist cabins. They called themselves "Reel California Girls" because they had worked in silent films in Hollywood as extras and in bit parts. It was rumored that the girls offered a bit more than the standard fare of Southern fried chicken and a comfortable bed. Virtually overnight, Vista Lodge became a favorite weekend night spot for both locals and visitors brave enough to travel the deadly curves of the canyon road. Unfortunately, the lodge burned to the ground in 1924, effectively closing this unusual and unique resort.

Priest Canyon Road closed in 1927 when the new road to the gorge was built, providing an easier, safer, and more direct route to the Royal Gorge. However, the new road also bypassed the incomparable views that briefly made Priest Canyon Road famous.

Words often fail us when we attempt to describe the emotions felt when being in Priest Canyon for the first time, but H. N. Beecher probably described these wonders for all of us when he wrote the following in the March 21, 1910 edition of the *Cañon City Times*:

"Each evening when the sun says its farewell to the wonders of the Royal Gorge hills; when coyotes from the high plains over in Jim Priest's pasture wail their evening vespers in the great unknown, foxes, wildcats and the wary mountain lion creep from their hiding places in the red rocks and leave footprints in the sands of Priest's Canyon. Yes, you can see things, hear things and dream them in this great beauty spot given by nature to the weary ones of Cañon City."

Today, much of Priest Canyon Road runs through privately-owned land, and permission must be sought to wander this "boulevard of beauty."

Ward Collection

The Jim Priest Ranch, 1895.

The Odd Fellows & Rebekah Home
1020 North Fifteenth Street

In today's age of questionable corporate practices, it is indeed odd to find a multi-million dollar organization predicated on "visiting the sick, relieving the distressed, burying the dead, and educating the orphan."

Such is the description of the Independent Order of Odd Fellows, or IOOF. Members consider themselves odd because they are dedicated to doing good and helping others. Their motto is simply the chain of friendship, love and truth. While their unusual name probably does not do much to promote all the good they have performed in Cañon City, they continue to quietly, and without fanfare, serve a community by touching the human heart.

The women's auxiliary of IOOF – the Rebekahs – also has a stellar history. The Colorado Chapter of The Rebekahs is the largest in the world, with its storied education assistance program being touted as one of the United States' most effective programs ever devised.

At first glance, the majestic Odd Fellows & Rebekah Home located on North Fifteenth Street appears as though it could have been constructed as part of a grand Southern estate. Built in 1914, the town's business leaders lobbied the IOOF to have the home built here, as they correctly perceived the financial benefits of such a building in the community. Similar to the Union Printers Home in Colorado Springs, the IOOF Home was built during the time when members were taken care of by their own if they became ill, poor, or were suddenly orphaned children of IOOF members. During this period in our country's history, there were no government-sponsored social programs or safety nets in place. It was left almost entirely to churches and fraternal organizations to care for the sick, the indigent and the disadvantaged.

In time, admission to the Odd Fellows Home included non-members.

The stately building cost approximately $50,000 when it was completed. Unlike any other building in town, its 13,470 square feet of inside space housed dormitories for the 154 boys and girls raised within its walls during its fifty-eight years as an orphanage. With its 128 windows and 115 doors, a library, dining rooms, playroom, sunrooms and kitchen, it could be a maze to navigate for new residents, several of whom still live in the surrounding community. But with the slow arrival of adoption and foster care laws in Colorado, the home began to accept fewer and fewer children, till there were none.

Today, the Odd Fellows & Rebekah Home serves the elderly, and it continues to be one of Cañon City's treasured buildings with a long, proven - and yes, odd – history of doing good by helping others.

Ward Collection

The Odd Fellows Home, 1925.

Colorado National Guard Company C
Annex Hall, Main Street

The Colorado National Guard has had a long and storied history in Cañon City, as various units have been instrumental in preserving the town's legacy as a defender of freedom since the days of the American Civil War.

They were called the First Colorado Regiment, a quickly formed group of local men organized into active duty in the early 1860s for the Union Army. They fought the Confederate forces at the Battle of Glorietta Pass, but disbanded soon after the completion of the war. They were renowned for their bravery under fire.

In 1887, a group of riflemen from Cañon City were recruited and designated as Company H, 2nd Infantry. Their purpose was to offer resistance to a group of Native Americans believed to be involved in an uprising following the needless shooting deaths of several members of their tribe by the military. This notorious incident became known as the Meeker Massacre. Almost ten years later, Company F, 2nd Infantry was formed. This unit was comprised of most of the soldiers from Company H, which had been mustered out in the same year of 1898. This company remained active until 1904.

By 1915, Company K, 2nd Infantry was organized in Cañon City, transferred to the 1st Infantry and later re-designated as Company C, 1st Colorado Infantry. The company drilled once a week at Annex Hall, which was located at the 600 block of Main Street, on the second floor of the Annex Building.

The date was June 22, 1916, and the Spanish American War was in full swing. Company C was about to receive a sendoff the likes of which Cañon City had not seen before, or since.

Mexico's rebel leader, Pancho Villa, in response to President Woodrow Wilson's endorsement of Mexico's new President Venustiano Carranzo, crossed the border into New Mexico and killed six Americans at an outpost in Columbus. Wilson then sent General John Pershing to the Mexican border to seek out and punish Villa. This journey came to be called "Pershing's Punitive Expedition". Many young American boys signed on with Pershing, including the newly formed Company C of the Colorado National Guard.

According to the *Daily Record*, as the troops gathered at the Denver & Rio Grande Railroad Depot preparing to depart, "It was the most wonderful, spontaneous outburst of patriotism ever

Ward Collection

Colorado National Guard Company C
being greeted by thousands of local well-wishers, June 22, 1916.

witnessed in Cañon City." More than three thousand citizens arrived to offer their support. The Cañon City Cornet Band and the High School Cadet Corps escorted the company to the train. Civic and church groups had fashioned small gift packets for each of the approximately fifty soldiers. And before the train began to pull away, many kisses, hugs, and tears were exchanged with wives, mothers, and girlfriends. Fathers bravely shook the hands of their young sons, many of whom had just graduated from high school days before. They were mere boys, untested by the world, and unfamiliar with the horrors of war.

After a brief period of training in Golden, Colorado, Pershing's troops headed out to capture Pancho Villa. Numerous border skirmishes ensued, but after several unsuccessful months into the campaign, President Wilson ordered the troops back home.

It is believed that all members of Company C of the Colorado National Guard returned back home to Cañon City without a single casualty.

Company C preparing to leave Cañon City on their mission to
Mexico, followed by the Cañon City Cornet Band, June 22, 1916.

Rudd Park
Twelfth Street and Rudd Avenue

Before Cañon City had motels, inns, and recreational vehicle camps, it had Rudd Park, the first official city-sponsored welcome mat to overnight visitors traveling in horseless carriages.

It was on June 18, 1917 that Cañon City purchased several city lots at Twelfth and Rudd for the grand sum of one thousand and five hundred dollars. It was flat, dry land with a few mature trees scattered about. But more importantly, those few trees provided much needed shade from the oppressive heat of the summer sun. The city council had hoped to convert the mostly barren ground into an early version of today's RV park. With Independence Day celebrations, the goal was to offer the casual visitor – not able to afford an expensive hotel room – a safe and comfortable place to stay for a week or more. The rationale given at the time was that the longer a visitor stayed in town, the more money they would likely spend while here. The logic was a sound one, as new visitors brought tents and camping equipment, and indeed, did extend their visits by weeks, not just days.

By the mid-1920s, several permanent cottages were hastily built at the park for those without tents or equipment, and were rented for one dollar a night. But the popularity of these odd little cottages was vastly underestimated, as many guests waited in long lines, for days on end, for an opportunity to rent one of the buildings. This dilemma was not lost on those of an entrepreneurial spirit. Within weeks several cottage motels began popping up all across town, overshadowing the Rudd Park cottages by offering running water and electricity. By the early 1930's, the Rudd Park cottages would cease to exist.

With the recreational cottage industry firmly in place, in 1934 the city pulled the welcome mat to motorized travelers to Rudd Park. They demolished the few remaining cottages and converted the land into a city playground, with a dedication on June 11, 1934. The playground had set hours of operation with a city supervisor to oversee the park's activities.

By the 1950's, Rudd Park had become neglected and ill-maintained, and in a very serious state of deterioration. However, by the 1960s, and with a newly-built high school across the street at College Avenue, community interest in the park once again took hold. Eventually, and in ensuing years, playground equipment was updated, tennis courts were built, and the Rotary Club provided basketball courts. And by the early 1990s, Cañon City High School students volunteered to help maintain Rudd Park.

Rudd Park was first envisioned to serve a community need, and almost a century later, that vision has evolved to include all that is before us today, with irrigated grounds, maintained equipment, numerous healthy shade trees, and a prideful neighborhood long grateful for the park's positive evolution.

Local History Center, Cañon City

Rudd Park, 1920.

The Jones Motion Picture Theatre
606 Main Street

At the turn of the twentieth century, the most popular form of entertainment was the silent movie house. Every week, literally millions of Americans eagerly paid a modest fee to view images thought to exist only in their dreams. Both adults and children would line up for blocks to see the latest drama, comedy, or Western hero. While the opera house next door delivered live drama and music, the movie house offered something unique and unchallenged: live Vaudeville acts, cinematic action and adventure, and an orchestra to accompany the screened film. Every night was a staged extravaganza, and few patrons were disappointed. The best part was that you could come back time and again and relive the Cowboy exploits of Tom Mix and Hoot Gibson, or mourn the fate of Lillian Gish. Such was the power of silent film.

The Jones Motion Picture Theatre was built in the Fall of 1917 by theater veteran Jesse Jones, who also acted as the theater's manager. With an unheard of cost of $40,000, it seemed no sum was spared in the building of the finest theater in the area. With white mahogany woodwork, stained and painted glass in the windows on the second floor, and a tiled roof, this art-deco theater was the pride of the community. Initially projected to seat one-thousand patrons in small, closely-placed chairs on both the main floor and balcony, by the time the theater was finished, the true figure was closer to six-hundred floor-bolted seats.

Sporting a seven-piece orchestra, the theater's opening night of April 19, 1918 was greeted with gleeful delight from both guests and the media. "The Kaiser – The Beast of Berlin" was screened to sell-out audiences every night for a full week. Film after film did similar business for months thereafter. During the few days when the circus came to town, the theater would be almost empty, so the enterprising theater owner would set up a 16mm silent film camera and film patrons as they entered the circus. Later the next day he would show his "circus film" to his patrons – but only during circus week. Word soon spread of Jones' stunt, and intrigued patrons felt compelled to follow-up their circus visit with a trip to the movie house. Jones was certain everyone wanted to see themselves up on the huge silver screen, and his ticket receipts for the week confirmed this.

Jesse Jones sold his theater to B. P. McCormick in 1925. The McCormick family owned several other nearby theaters, so they were well-acquainted with the nature of the business. Innovative and enterprising, they were one of the first movie house owners to offer talking pictures to the public as

The Jones Motion Picture Theatre, 1922.

early as 1929, and were paramount in bringing quality cinema to Cañon City during the "golden age" of filmmaking in the 1930s and 1940s. It was also in the early 1940s that they changed the name of the theater to the Skyline Theater, in honor of Skyline Drive. And as long-time owners, they personally witnessed the decline of the theater attendance in the 1960s and 1970s.

Finally, in 2001, Harold McCormick sold his beloved theater to Chuck and Marianne James. The Jameses were local owners who loved saving old movie houses, and they did just that with the Skyline. Over a period of nine long months, the Skyline Theater was painstakingly restored to its former glory, but with fewer seats for the overall comfort of the customer, and boasting a $40,000 Dolby Digital sound system. The Skyline Theater was back to stay, and its re-opening (with the film "Pearl Harbor") was attended by the McCormick family, who found favor with its restoration.

Amazingly, the Skyline Theater, for more than eighty years, has always existed only as a motion picture house. This fine and wonderful building has become one of downtown Cañon City's crowning jewels.

This movie still is from the film *Over the Santa Fe Trail*, starring Noel Neill.
It was first shown in Cañon City in 1947. Literally thousands of films
have been screened at the Skyline Theatre since 1918.

The Pepper Creamery Company
408 Main Street

Very little is known about the The Pepper Creamery Company, shown in this photograph of 1920. Operating at this Main Street site from 1918 to 1923, the company was one of the few merchants of dairy products in Cañon City, selling their own brand of Perfection butter and ice cream. Although small by today's standards, they did manage to produce more than six-hundred pounds of rich, creamy butter on a daily basis. Their primary customers were first other merchants such as restaurants and hotels, then town residents. Customers could either stop by the shop for goods, or arrange for home delivery, which most opted for. Owing to the plight of the lack of speedy public transportation, citizens soon learned that attempting to transport ice cream home via horse or on foot proved to be a highly unrewarding and disappointing experience. With the company's delivery truck equipped with an insulated, ice-filled compartment, dairy products could easily be made available to awaiting customers with nary a loss in texture or quality.

The building at 408 Main Street is thought to have been built between the years of 1890 and 1895 by J. E. Weaver and E. D. Bond, to house their fresh meat market and cold storage shop.

Later merchants to occupy this address were the Crust-O-Gold Bakery from 1931 to 1932; the Elk Café from 1946 to 1960; the Health–Aid Mart in 1964; Vic's TV Service in 1966; and Lasting Impressions in 1982.

The Pepper Creamery Company, 1920.

The Jewett Fire Brick Company
Eleventh And Royal Gorge Boulevard

Ernst Ford Jewett, along with Sarah A. McRay and Dr. Mary Phelps, started Jewett Fire Brick Company on South Ninth Street in 1900. It was one of the few predominately female–administrated businesses in Colorado. A woman running a high-profile business was not a wholly accepted concept during this era. Most female executives would offer just the initials of their first and middle names on documents and public filings, so that their gender would not encourage bias against them.

By 1917, although the company was successful, profitable, and respected in the community, Ernst had some difficulty getting along with his partners, so he prepared the groundwork for his own brick yard two blocks away on Eleventh and Water Street (later changed to Royal Gorge Boulevard). He favorably negotiated the rights to use his name on the new facility, so the Ninth Street brick yard's name was changed to The Diamond Fire Brick Company.

The new Jewett Fire Brick Company was completed and running at full capacity by 1918. Much of the clay for their bricks came from the hogbacks near Skyline Drive. The bricks were of such high quality that both railroad depots, as well as Alquin Hall Dormitory at the Holy Cross Abbey, were built from Jewett bricks.

Through Ernst Jewett's direction, Jewett Fire Brick Company quickly became one of Cañon City's most prized companies – that is, until Ernst's untimely death in the mid-1930s. Without his astute guidance, the plant closed in 1938 and was not reopened until 1943. Pioneer Brick Works, owned by the husband of one of Ernst's daughters, operated the yard only until 1946, when, once again, it closed. The Freeman Firebrick Company purchased the plant in 1949, but sold it to Harbison Walker in 1957, who continued operations until 1968. In the same year, Ferd Mueller, an engineer at the plant, purchased the facility and renamed it the Colorado Refractories Corporation. Ferd and Jeanne Mueller, happily lead the popular and innovative company to annual gross revenues of up to three million dollars, with a dedicated and specialized staff of thirty employees.

In 1990 Colorado Refractories Corporation was sold to Adience, Inc., at the time, a Pittsburgh-based corporation. The new owners changed its name to BMI Colorado Refractories Division. The plant continued operations until 2000.

Today, the brick yard at 309 South Eleventh Street is vacant. However, the remains of the original plant of 1918 are still quite visible.

The Jewett Fire Brick Company, C. 1948.

The Lithia Bottling Company
308 Main Street

The Lithia Bottling Company was a brilliant, but short-lived, enterprise by proprietor J.M. Egan in the early 1920s. Using water from the nearby Soda Springs, Lithia was able to bottle and market their own popular brands of soda, syrup, and crushed fruits. Their market served the Cañon City area.

The company's name was derived from the mineral water that contains lithium salts. According to Webster's, lithium is a "soft silver-white univalent element of the alkali metal group that is the lightest metal known and this is used especially in nuclear reactions and metallurgy."

Unfortunately, it is believed that in 1928 an analysis of the water at Soda Springs was performed, and while many healthful minerals were found, it was also determined that the water was radioactive.

The building at 308 Main Street was built in 1886. Originally a grocery and general household goods store, it was soon occupied by Higgins Brothers Second Hand Goods Store from 1903 to 1913, and by McIlvaney & Higgins Furniture & Carpet Cleaning Business in 1917. Both businesses were owned by the colorful Elwood "Woody" Higgins, who gained local fame for providing horses for several Tom Mix movies filmed by the Selig Movie Company in Cañon City in 1911 and 1912.

After Lithia's short stay in Cañon City, the building later became the home of Uncle Tom's A-1 Furniture Store, and Miss Eva Berney's Millinery Shop. The Royal Order of The Moose owned the brick building for several decades thereafter, eventually passing it on to Master Printers in 1978. Master Printers has occupied the building since 1950.

The Lithia Bottling Company, 1922.

Libby, McNeill, & Libby
Third And Royal Gorge Boulevard

By the late 19th century, Cañon City's reputation as the regional leader in fruit and vegetable farming was unchallenged. In the December 1895 edition of *Arid America*, a "national journal devoted to irrigation and descriptive of the West," the editors gushed that area farmers produced huge quantities of raspberries, gooseberries, blackberries, strawberries, grapes, cantaloupes, tomatoes, string beans, cherries, apples, plums, peaches, pears, apricots, corn, wheat and alfalfa – all on approximately two-thousand acres of rich, fertile soil. In fact, by the early 1920s, area farmers were raising and shipping literally millions of dollars worth of high quality produce annually. Such production attracted the likes of the nationally renowned pickle firm, Libby, McNeill & Libby of Chicago, which set up a warehouse and shipping station at Third And Water Streets, where the parking lot of the tourist train is now located.

While most of the large orchards of that era are but a faint memory to us today, many of Cañon City's backyards still show evidence of a once-striving industry. From North Cañon to the boundaries of the city, a relatively large number of homeowners still happily gather bushels of apricots, peaches, plums, and apples. They are the almost-forgotten remnants of a time when the orchard was king, and most of the city's residents labored in the fields next to their modest homes. It was a time when an apple stirred our souls and the crunch, juice and tartness made us long for the harvest. The orchard often was a wonderful and timeless place, filled with the memories of our ancestors of long ago.

Readying pickle barrels for loading onto railroad train cars, 1920.

The State Armory
110 Main Street

The State Armory building has long been regarded as the home of the Colorado Army National Guard, with seemingly endless numbers of personnel carriers, tanks and other vehicles parked within its grounds. But to generations of Cañon City residents, the State Armory has been the source of memories far more personal and wide-ranging.

Designed by architect John James Huddart of Denver, the armory was built in 1922 by inmate labor from the Territorial Prison, just a short walk away. With a budget of forty-thousand dollars, twelve talented masons constructed this handsome 3,840 square foot brick, stone and cement building. Although it is the longest continuously used armory in Colorado, its use as an armory has been overshadowed by its use as a local community center. Almost from the day the doors of this Mediterranean Revival-styled building were first opened, the armory has hosted dozens of high profile community events. In the 1920s and 1930s, automobile shows displayed the newest Packards, Cords, Pierce-Arrows, Studebakers, Cadillacs and Chevrolets. Flower shows and 4-H Club craft and poultry shows were almost annual events in the armory as early as the 1930s. And as many long-time residents fondly recall, from 1923 to 1960, the building was home to Cañon City High School Tigers basketball games, high school dances, and many graduation ceremonies. Although the building was first touted as seating as many as fifteen hundred individuals, through time and remodeling, perhaps half that number could comfortably be seated in the armory today.

As an unknowing tribute to Cañon City's pioneering silent movie-making days from 1910 to 1914, the State Armory will long be known as one of the sites for the production of several popular films. Scott Brady's 1948 prison film, *Cañon City*, was filmed here, as was 1969's *True Grit* with John Wayne and Kim Darby, and Goldie Hawn's *The Dutchess & the Dirtwater Fox* in 1976.

The Rolling Stones came calling in 1971 – no, not early live theater and vaudeville performer Fred Stone and his family known as the Rolling Stones, but that quaint British musical combo – although no photographs of their visit seem to exist. And even the World Wrestling Federation used the armory in the 1980s for several staged events.

The exterior of the State Armory has changed very little since 1922. The building continues to serve a proud community grateful for its long-standing presence.

The State Armory
First and Main Streets, C. 1940.

Ward Collection

Lobby card for the 1948 movie filmed at the Armory, "Canon City."

The 4-H Club Craft and Poultry Show at the Armory, C. 1930.

The Round Crest Canning Company
Eighth Street And Royal Gorge Boulevard

Built in 1898, this large building was the original home of the Colorado Canning Company and Jones Brothers Company, both of which shared the same building and competed against one another in the preserving of various fruits and vegetables.

Percy H. Troutman, who owned a large apple orchard in Fruitmere, which is now part of the Holy Cross Abbey, purchased the property in 1912 and started two companies, the Round Crest Canning Company, and the Colorado Fruit Company. In 1923, he consolidated both companies and changed the Round Crest brand name (which produced the "Green Hill" and "Skyline" labels) to the Colorado Packing Corporation.

Although news articles at the time described the canning company as being modern in every way, and with every comfort, there was probably very little comfort to be found for those who worked there. As the accompanying photographs would indicate, work was hard; it was performed in close quarters without air conditioning, and often during the hottest of days. For many employees, it was not the best of times, yet these companies did provide much needed income to thousands of men and women of the region. And during the apple harvest seasons between 1890 and 1930, canning companies employed so many workers that schools were often closed in order to accommodate the need for labor.

Troutman, who had an elaborate home at 902 Greenwood Avenue, turned over the operation of his company to the Colorado State Prison in 1925, with the state eventually purchasing it in 1927. The state continued to work out of the building in one capacity or another until 1974, when it was razed, ending the building's seventy-six year contribution to the community. Ultimately, both the building and the fruit industry became victims of growth and land development.

Local History Center, Cañon City

Round Crest Canning Company, 1917.

Local History Center, Cañon City

Peeling apples on the production line.
Round Crest Canning Company, 1917.

The Round Crest Canning Company, 1917.

The Suspension Bridge
The Royal Gorge

The Suspension Bridge at the Royal Gorge is a bridge that leads to nowhere. It serves no true utilitarian purpose, appears to have little social value, and is located in an area that encourages a fear of heights.

However, the Royal Gorge Suspension Bridge is also the third most visited tourist attraction in Colorado (right behind Rocky Mountain National Park and the Air Force Academy), and since 1929, it has been responsible for pouring millions of dollars into the local economy.

The Royal Gorge was originally called the Grand Canyon of the Arkansas, but the name was changed in the 1870s so it would not be confused with Arizona's Grand Canyon. In 1906, primarily through the efforts of the *Cañon City Record*'s Guy Hardy, Congress conveyed to Cañon City five thousand acres in and around the gorge as a park. But as early as 1900 visionaries seriously ruminated about building a bridge that would span the edges of the gorge. One group of entrepreneurs at the turn of the century offered stock certificates for the "Cañon City-Florence and Royal Gorge Interurban Railway CO." On the face of the certificate was a drawing of an automobile crossing a bridge at the gorge. And while Coronado first documented a visit to the gorge in 1540 during his search for gold, and Zebulon Pike and his small band of explorers camped nearby and entered the canyon in 1806, it was not until the sudden appearance of a lavish article in the June 1906 edition of *Technical World* that the nation first became aware of the economic possibilities of the Royal Gorge. The article was typical of the era, with line after line of hyperbolic descriptions of things to come. The writer confidently states that a newly-constructed glass bridge would be twenty-two feet in width, 2,627 feet above the Arkansas River, and be completed by midsummer of 1906 at a cost of $100,000.

The writer of that article was wrong on all counts.

Twenty-three years later – on June 25, 1929 – work began in earnest on the building of the Royal Gorge Suspension Bridge. Financed by Lon P. Piper of Texas, the Royal Gorge Bridge and Amusement Co. was formed to finally construct this bridge of dreams. Hiring Houston engineer George E. Cole, and with a workforce of about eighty men, the company completed this engineering feat by December of 1929.

When the bridge was completed, the final cost came to $350,000. Workmen were paid between thirty to sixty cents per hour, ten hours a day, seven days a week – without a single casualty or serious injury. Rather than glass, the bridge was built of steel with 1,292 wood planks. It is eighteen feet wide, and rises 1,053 feet above the river.

As a footnote to this historic event, when the bridge was dedicated on December 6, 1929, three thousand individuals gathered for the celebration, including young Estelle Ann Smith and her beau, Sam Argus. They were the first couple married at the bridge that day. Since that time, both literally and figuratively, dozens of others have also taken the plunge.

Finally, still acclaimed as the world's highest suspension bridge, in 2004 the Royal Gorge Suspension Bridge was named by the American Council of Engineering Companies of Colorado as one of Colorado's most significant bridges – although it continues to be a bridge that leads to nowhere.

Ward Collection

The Suspension Bridge at the Royal Gorge, 1930.

The Rotary Club

The Rotary Club of Cañon City has been an almost permanent fixture in the community since the early 1930s. A service organization dedicated to the worldwide eradication of polio, the club locally is comprised of about seventy members whose varied backgrounds are of a professional nature, such as business owners and persons in positions of authority.

First established by Paul Harris in Chicago in 1905, The Rotary Club is an international organization with 29,000 clubs located in 159 countries. Notoriously media-shy, local members have quietly donated Cañon City's first fire and rescue truck, organized the nativity scene atop Skyline Drive, built the basketball courts west of the Cañon City High School, and provided funds for the construction of the 500-pound Cloister Court replica fountain in Veterans Park.

As Cañon City grows and progresses, there is little doubt that the Rotary Club will continue to be a supportive hand in the town's development, and offer solutions to its many social needs.

Oct. 9. 1935

The Rotary Club of 1935.

Cañon City Schools

Often forgotten in the telling of a town's local history is the story of the development of its education system. Cañon City's story is one filled with great promise, a little disappointment, and much success.

Prior to the city's incorporation in 1872, schools in the area were essentially for-profit institutions privately owned and operated on a tuition basis. For those not affording such luxury – which was most of the population – education came by way of home schooling. Later, churches and local community centers offered group learning for children of differing ages to be taught by parents, ministers and volunteers – and by one another.

By 1866, Cañon City citizens formed District #1, the area's first formal school district. It would be the first of no fewer than forty-five separate and distinct school districts in Fremont County. Before the advent of the horseless carriage, travel of any distance greater than two miles was rare for most county residents, so each small community would develop their own district to serve the needs of their children.

Cañon City's first public school building was an older structure known locally as Bates Hall. Located at 518 Main Street, and first used in 1870, the school's first teacher was Nellie Virden Morford. With an initial enrollment of twelve students, this small two-story building served as the town's central education center for ten years, until the district built its first modern school building in 1880. At a cost of $13,472, the Public School, as it was called, was built at the six-hundred block of Macon Avenue, on the very spot where the County Administration Building now sets. Later named Washington School, the facility had neither plumbing or electricity during the early years of use.

In his highly detailed and well-written 1997 book, *All Hail The Tigers*, local educator Bruce Sherwood documents that Washington School housed all grades, from primary school to high school, and "one of the early rules was that any student carrying a gun to school was subject to expulsion." Apparently, not much has changed in that area of education more than a century later.

Washington School continued to serve as an elementary school until 1950, when a new elementary school was built at Ninth Street and College Avenue in 1952. With a seeming lack of creativity, it, too, was named Washington School. Since that time, the 1880 building is now referred to as Old Washington, and the 1952 building as New Washington. Similar confusion resulted when referencing

Girls Basketball Team of Cañon City High School
at Old Washington School, 1899.

Lincoln School, since there have been two such schools in the district: the 1894 "Old" Lincoln School that was located on the northeast corner of Fourteenth and Main Streets – and educated many of the children from the Odd Fellows Home – on the spot that is now the home of the District Administration Building; and "New" Lincoln, located on Myrtle Avenue in South Cañon, built in 1952.

As a high school, Old Washington School graduated 151 students between 1885 and 1902, when a new school was built to educate only high school students. Also located on Ninth Street and College Avenue, the new Cañon City High School was touted as the most modern high school in the state. In addition to a chemistry laboratory, and biology and physics departments, the basement also contained two bowling alleys, "dedicated specifically to use by young women, an armory for the cadets and athletic showers." By 1916, an annex building was constructed at Tenth Street and College Avenue as both a manual training building, and the district's high school gymnasium.

Cañon City has had a long and documented history of not adequately foreseeing the educational needs of the community by underfunding the school district, or waiting years too late to act on immediate needs, often resulting in overcrowding and outdated facilities. And so it was in 1925, after skyrocketing enrollment – due primarily to the consolidation with South Cañon in 1920 – that a new, larger high school was finally built between the twelve-hundred and fourteen-hundred blocks of Main Street. Designed for 450 students, this beautiful building served the city well, graduating 4,244 students from 1925 to 1961. When the high school at 1313 College Avenue was constructed, this fine old high school became known as Cañon City Junior High School, then (in 1988) Cañon City Middle School.

The original Cañon City High School at Ninth Street and College Avenue later became Roosevelt Junior High School. It served in that capacity from 1925 until 1969, when it was razed.

It was a time for rejoicing and a time to celebrate, when the new Cañon City High School was opened in September of 1961. Long, sleek, and low in appearance, the ultra modern complex built on thirty-three acres finally conveyed to students all of the physical amenities of the time, including a large gymnasium, several science laboratories, and a foreign language and photography laboratory. The school also sported a brand new single telephone line and two telephones.

In the years to follow, classrooms were added, as was a new athletic field. Vocational education programs were expanded, computers were requisitioned, and a new 450-seat performing arts center was constructed.

But as many long-time residents will recall, Cañon City high school has not stood alone as the only high school in the area. It is extraordinary that residents have supported as many as five separate high schools in a town with a relatively small population. In addition to Cañon City High School, the other high schools in the area were South Cañon High School, Colorado Collegiate & Military Institute, Mount St. Scholastica Academy, and the Abbey School.

Local History Center, Cañon City

Nellie Virden Morford,
Cañon City's first public school teacher, 1880.

Local History Center, Cañon City

Old Washington School, the first public school building
constructed in Cañon City in 1880.

Local History Center, Cañon City

Kindergarten class, Old Washington School, 1888.
Back Row, Left to Right: Rose Beecher, Will Waldo, Julia Arbuckle,
Vera Teape, Claudia Teape, May Harding, Lou Beecher.
Middle Row: Ted Harding, Ruth Webster, Jeanie Whipple, Ruth Lewis, Fritz Raynolds.
Bottom Row: Gretchen Harding, Harmon Minor, George Bethel, Edna Robinson.

Local History Center, Cañon City

Cañon City High School Class of 1888,
at Old Washington School.

Old Washington School
Kate Bartlett's Eighth Grade Class
1890-1891
Top Row: Alex McDaniels, Bert McDaniels, Laura McDaniels, Joe McKeeham,
Kate Bartlett, Jimmie Peabody, Emma Pearce, Charles Bockerra, Emma Bocking.
Second Row: Maude Chapman, Nellie Chapman, Bobby Fletcher, Cline Fletcher,
June Brewster, Bill McClure, Harry Chambers, Cora Shank.
Third Row: Jimmy Wright, Olive Wright, Aida Wright, Geo Murphy,
Elise Helm, Bob Hagan, Stella Roberts, Charles Logan.
Bottom Row: Hunter Winkley, Mille Wacker, Mary Phelps, Grace Fletcher,
Sarah Allison, Maude Campbell, Frank Pennington, Fred Wilson, Mary Renny.

Local History Center, Cañon City

Cañon City High School Graduating Class of 1895
at Old Washington School.
It was the first class to successfully complete all twelve grades.
Top: Charles Shaeffer, Winnifred Coombs, Professor Scott, Victoria Rudolph, Fred Wilson
Front: Principal Belle Minor, George Wells, Olive Wright, Amelia Wacker,
Professor J. H. Allen (later Superintendent of Schools), Amos Jones.

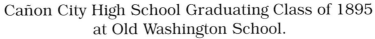

Faculty, staff, and the student body of
Old Washington School, 1901-1902.

Local History Center, Cañon City

Old Lincoln School at 14th and Main Streets in Cañon City.
Seventh and Eighth grades, C. 1895.

This large building - the finest public school building in the state
at the time - was Cañon City High School from 1902 to 1925.
Located at Ninth Street and College Avenue, it later became
Roosevelt Junior High School from 1925 to 1969.
The location is now the home of "New" Washington Elementary School.

Cañon City High School Baseball Team, 1915.
Top Row, Left to Right: Kerfy Corrin, Finis Parks, Professor George,
Jim McClintock, Roy Erickson, Professor T. D. Harris, Ed Sharman, Walter Boyle.
Bottom Row: Harl Tanner, Bill Rabshall, Bill Kennedy,
George O'Bryan, Tim Walsh, George Matkin.

Cañon City High School Basketball Team, 1915.
Top Row: Phil Wilkens, Professor George, Fred Merriam, Finis Parks,
Ed Sharman, Professor T. D. Harris, Walter Lauterbach.
Bottom Row: Richard Johnson, Bill Kennedy, Jim McClintock,
Bill Rabshall, George Matkin.

Local History Center, Cañon City

Student Council, Cañon City High School, 1925.
Top Row, Left to Right: C. G. Smith, Science; L. L. Beahm, Principal; H. E. Small, Science;
Edith Hamilton Childears, English; Winifred Rhodes Shouse; Charles Lafferty.
Middle Row: Henry Paul; Herbert Benson; Nancy Pleasants Anderson;
Agnes Benson Bjornlie; Edith Landers; Lee Walker; Jeston Meyer.
Front Row: R. J. Woodward; Thelma Owens King; Virginia Drinkwater;
Bertha Brackney Stampfel; Mary Margaret Cooper Pavey.

This building served as Cañon City High School from 1925 to 1961.
Located at 1215 Main Street, it is now Cañon City Middle School.

Local History Center, Cañon City

Cañon City High School, 1313 College Avenue, 1961.

SOUTH CAÑON HIGH SCHOOL

In terms of both academics and athletics, South Cañon High School was always "North" Cañon High School's main rival. Located south of the Arkansas and west of Ninth Street, South Cañon's School District #8 was formed in 1871, with an old log cabin on South Ninth Street being its first schoolhouse. After several false starts, a new school building was constructed in 1885 and named Prospect Street School. In 1887 its name was changed to the Fourth Street School. The district then added a high school program to the Fourth Street School in 1889, with twenty students enrolling in its three-year course of study. The school name was again changed in 1891 to Alcott School, then (finally) changed once again in 1925 to Garfield Elementary.

In 1904, owing to a sudden population boom due mostly to mining and fruit farming, and at a cost of fifteen-thousand dollars, District #8 built a separate high school at 1104 Park Avenue in Lincoln Park. Prideful and enthusiastic, this small but determined student body excelled in all things academic, coupled with championship athletic teams to cheer for.

Unfortunately, it all came to an end on the evening of November 14, 1914 when the high school was gutted by a devastating fire. It was quickly rebuilt, but the high school program lasted only until 1920 when the school graduated its final ten students. With a suddenly declining population, South Cañon School District #8 reluctantly consolidated with Cañon City's District #1. The high school building became Wilson Junior High School in 1921, then an elementary school in 1962. It was eventually sold in 1970 and converted into apartments.

Local History Center, Cañon City

The South Cañon School of many names:
Prospect Street School (1885), Fourth Street School (1889),
Alcott School (1891), and Garfield Elementary (1925).
These images were taken in 1885.

Local History Center, Cañon City

Eighth Grade, Alcott School, 1908.
Back Row, Left to Right: Fred McKinley, Earl Serry, Katie Sidford, Grace Lovell,
Miss Eldora Britt (Teacher), Nona Nelchi, Martha Logan, Unidentified.
Second Row, Left to Right: Fay Ewell, Ada Blakeslee,
Mildren Bryant, Florence Gerlach, Maude Mack.
Front Row, Left to Right: Minnie Snyder, Eddie Ashton,
George Grundman, Bill Watt, John Griffen, Edith Miller.

South Cañon High School, 1909. It was built in 1904.

South Cañon High School Athletic Team, C. 1905.

South Cañon High School Girls Basketball Team, 1914.
Tow Row: Sylvia Gaines, Jessie Pringle, Bethrel Miller, Ruth McKinley
Bottom Row: Dorris Ewall, Clara Jefferson, Jane Lewis

Local History Center, Cañon City

Local History Center, Cañon City

South Cañon High School destroyed by fire on November 14, 1914.

South Cañon High School was rebuilt in 1915, but the new building
served as a high school only until 1920, when it was then called
Wilson Junior High. It remained as Wilson until 1961.
In 1970 it was converted into apartments. This photograph was taken in 1922.

Local History Center, Cañon City

The 1920 Freshman Class of South Cañon High School.
These students were among the last high school students to attend
South Cañon High School. The school closed in the same year.

COLORADO COLLEGIATE AND MILITARY INSTITUTE

The year was 1880, and through the work of several Union Army veterans and the Grand Army of the Republic, and with Colorado Governor Frederick W. Pilkin in attendance, the cornerstone for the new Colorado Collegiate and Military Institute was laid.

The military school was an ambitious project, and it was armed with a board of trustees consisting of Cañon City's most powerful, most wealthy, and most influential citizens, with such names as Raynolds, Rudd, Rockafellow, Phelps, and Peabody. It was believed that with the governor as chancellor, and with local backing, it could not fail – but fail it did.

The military institute opened on December 1, 1881 with an enrollment of sixty-six cadets. Initially proposed to be an all-boys school, planners quickly understood that the region was simply too small to attract the number of male recruits needed for financial stability. So with a stroke of a pen, young women were also recruited. With an enormous tuition cost of $300 for the forty-week school session, it became a school for the wealthy and the elite with students attending from all across Colorado, as well as from England, North Wales, Kentucky, Kansas, Michigan and Pennsylvania.

Eligibility for admittance in the military school was not highly stringent. All you had to do was read, write, and speak English, be six years of age or older, know a little math, and abstain from alcohol while at school. Revelry commenced at 6:00 a.m. daily, and after chapel at 9:00 a.m., the remainder of the day was spent in study and contemplation – and attending cadet drills. For most students, it was a strict and structured, but comfortable environment.

Almost from its first day of existence, the school was in financial duress, and by 1884, it sought and received a $100,000 endowment from the Grand Army of the Republic. Moved by such a generous gift, the board of trustees voted to change the institution's name to the Grand Army Collegiate and Military Institute.

The financial gift did not significantly alleviate the school's troubles, and in 1885, Cañon City's military school was quietly closed and moved to the corner of Welton and 25th Streets in Denver, where it opened for classes on January 7, 1886. Upon its closure, the school building and property in Cañon City reverted back to its previous owners, the Central Colorado Improvement Company, owned by Fred Raynolds, James Campbell and William McClure. They, in turn, sold the property to Mary Virginia Macon, wife of local attorney Thomas Macon, on June 22, 1886 for twelve-thousand dollars.

Local History Center, Cañon City

Laying the cornerstone for the
Colorado Collegiate and Military Institute, 1880.

Local History Center, Cañon City

Male cadets at the Colorado Collegiate
and Military Institute, 1882.

This photograph is a rare print of the 1883 Class of Female Cadets,
The Colorado Collegiate and Military Institute.
Top Row: Kate Ashby, Eloise Lemons, Minnie Mack, Myrtle McClure,
Sara Trazer, Minnie Rickard, Ida Barber, Hawah Pedley.
Middle Row: Olive Sawyer, Nelle Alling, Faurie Bowlby, Carrie Locke,
Sadie Feltch, Addie Baldwin, Miss Larabie, Unidentified child.
Front Row: Mary Pedley, Mottie Logan, Unidentified, Unidentified, Miss Odell, Mary Phelps.

MOUNT ST. SCHOLASTICA ACADEMY

The Benedictine Sisters of Chicago journeyed to Breckenridge, Colorado in 1886 to operate St. Joseph's Hospital in this silver mining town on the Blue River. In quick order they opened a boys and girls school, St. Gertrude's Academy. The school thrived until the price of silver plunged, forcing most of the town's inhabitants to seek employment elsewhere, and in 1890, forcing the closure of St. Gertrude's Academy. But under the guidance of Bishop Nicholas Matz of Denver, the Sisters were encouraged to start a new school in Cañon City.

On May 14, 1890, the Benedictine Sisters bought the building and grounds of the vacant military school from Mary Virginia Macon for fifteen-thousand dollars. They made improvements to the large three-story building, and the former military school was reopened under the new name of Mount St. Scholastica Academy in September of 1890. It was now a private girls boarding school.

With a teaching staff of four nuns and a principal, all went well with the school until 1895 when the building was all but destroyed in a blast that blew out windows, cracked walls and unsettled the roof. Workers digging a tunnel under the hogback of nearby Skyline Drive apparently used more explosives than needed, with disastrous results. Almost immediately, students were sent home, and after much legal haggling, the state conveyed upon the school a small cash settlement and a commitment to have the school rebuilt by inmate labor from the Territorial Prison.

The school was reopened two years later in 1897. In the same year, a chapel was built by Eugene Reilly of Chicago. By 1900, the chaplain's cottage was completed, and in the late 1930s, "Mount" was removed from the school's name.

In the ensuing years, yearly enrollment increased to as many as 150 girls, necessitating the construction of additional buildings and other facilities.

St. Scholastica Academy finally closed its doors in 2002, after serving the educational needs of students worldwide for more than one hundred years.

Local History Center, Cañon City

Mount Saint Scholastica Academy, 1922.

THE ABBEY SCHOOL

Cañon City has always attracted those seeking a better life, or a better understanding of the life they live. So when the Benedictine Order from Pennsylvania bought Captain B.F. Rockafellow's apple orchard in Fruitmere in 1923, nary an eyebrow was raised. A group of monks set up quarters in Rockafellow's old apple house, and by 1925, broke ground for what was to become Holy Cross Abbey, soon to be the largest and most ornate privately-owned building in town.

With the Vatican's approval, and with an astounding budget of $500,000, the Abbey was completed and dedicated in April of 1926. By September, the Order also opened a boys' boarding school with thirty-seven first-year students. Room, board, and tuition were provided at a cost of three-hundred dollars per school year. While most of these boys were day students who lived in town, those who were boarders lived in the monastery. With enrollment almost doubling in 1927, a new spacious residence hall was constructed in 1928.

Over the years many new buildings were added – about one dozen in total – with the main building being the largest. At five stories in height, and with over one-hundred rooms, it stands as a monumental achievement in an unlikely setting.

Unfortunately, by 1984, even with a tuition fee reaching almost nine-thousand dollars, administrative costs were exceeding revenue. The student population for that year had dwindled to 133 students (with only 60 boarders) down from its 1977-1978 high of 244 students. So in 1985, after fifty-nine years of operation as a private high school, the Abbey School closed.

Ward Collection

Holy Cross Abbey, C. 1930.

Cañon City
Colorado

•••••

Brief Snapshots...

Campfire Girls, 1930.
Back Row, Left to Right: Nell Knauff Cathram, Dorothy Maynard Chapman, Clara Jane Hollaway.
Front Row: Elvira Norman Brown, Edith Knauff, Gertrude Rogers Schooley, Marie Knauff Granthern,
Agnes Stinemeyer Hougland, Dores Norman Prigge, Vivian Wallen, Edna Rae Webb Moody, Dora Bedell Bowers.
Elvira Brown was the Guardian.

Local History Center, Cañon City

Local History Center, Cañon City

The Cañon City Cycle Club of 1896 consisted primarily of older males
in dark suits with flashy ties and a variety of headwear. By 1898, the same club
was made up primarily of young women in long coats and large hats.

The Cañon City Composer's Club, C. 1900.
Top Row, Left to Right: Mrs. R. Lewis, Mrs. John Cleghorn, William Eltrich, Queen Palmer.
Second Row: Eleanor Jenkins, Miss Snyder, Mrs. Stewart, Miss Davis, Miss Mackein,
Grace Dale, Mrs. T. M. Harding, Daisy Tenbrook, Anna Russel, Miss Briggs.
Third Row: Mrs. Fred Raynolds, Mr. Cox, Leon Wiedon, Jack Palmer, Mrs. Gibson, Pansy Reynolds.
Fourth Row: Mrs. Smith, Miss Wolf, Mary Phelps, Laura Green.

Veterans of Wars, May 1, 1921 – attending the Blossom Festival.
Top Row, Left to Right: A. J. Holesworth ("The Phillipines");
JROTC Cadet J. K. Emmerson; Paul Gillespie, Veteran of WWI.
Bottom Row: G. K. Tanner, Confederate Soldier; B. F. Rockafellow, Union Soldier.

Local History Center, Cañon City

The Cañon City Horseshoe Club of 1921.

Local History Center, Cañon City

Cañon City's Madison School in 1928,
with teacher Helen Pauls.

Situated on the Northwest corner of First and Main Streets,
this building is the former home of the Deputy Warden of the Territorial Prison.
It was built in 1901 on the spot where the old Fremont House was located.
The Fremont was a combination hotel, general store, and post office that existed
from 1860 to the 1890s. The Deputy Warden's home was heated by steam
piped in from the other side of the prison's wall.
This photograph was taken in 1922.

Located in South Cañon on First Street and built in the 1880s,
this 1892 photograph of the home of Cañon City businessman,
Lyman Robison, displayed Mr. Robison's obvious wealth as a
bank president and owner of mining interests.

Local History Center, Cañon City

Friends Jane Swanton and Jessie Eva Hartwel, C. 1890.

Ward Collection

An unidentified snowy street in Cañon City in 1909.

629 Harrison Avenue, 1909.
It was known as the First Christian Church of Cañon City.
At a cost of sixteen-thousand dollars, this cream-colored brick building with
its elaborate dome and Greek style of architecture, first began serving a
congregation of two hundred in the year of its construction, 1907.
It is now the home of the Vineyard Christian Fellowship.

Local History Center, Cañon City

The Harrison Family, 901 River Street (now Royal Gorge Boulevard), C. 1900.

The following words were written on the back of this photograph:

"(The) home of Henry and Mary Harrison...built in 1881 and purchased by the Harrisons in 1884. Henry and Mary are in the carriage, son Frank standing near them. Their daughters Edith and Ida are in the front yard.

Henry died in 1922 and Mary continued to live there until her death in 1930. The house was then occupied by daughter Ida, her husband James Hawthorne, and their son James Harrison Hawthorne.

Ida went to live in a local rest home in 1974 and the house was unoccupied for five years. It was finally demolished in 1979. Ida died in 1984, age 103 years."

Cañon City
Colorado

—•••—

The Changing Face of
Cañon City's Main Street
From 1884 to 1967.

Looking East

The 200 Block of Main Street, Looking East, 1886.

The 400 Block of Main Street, Looking East, 1919.

The 300 Block of Main Street, Looking East, 1928.

Ward Collection

The 600 Block of Main Street, Looking East, 1959.

Looking West

The 500 Block of Main Street, Looking West, 1884.

Local History Center, Cañon City

The 500 Block of Main Street, Looking West, 1905.

Ward Collection

The 600 Block of Main Street, Looking West, 1910.

The 600 Block of Main Street, Looking West, 1911.

The 600 Block of Main Street, Looking West, 1932.

The 600 Block of Main Street, Looking West, 1940.

The 600 Block of Main Street, Looking West, 1967.

Cañon City
Colorado

— • • • —

Acknowledgements

Acknowledgments

Writing this book was a wonderful and rewarding experience. At every step along the way, I met or worked with some genuinely kind and caring people who went out of their way to accommodate me in my quest for information about the early days of Cañon City.

Left to Right: LaDonna L. Gunn, Seth Adams, Natalie K. Bard, Susan K. Cochran, Teri A. Poston.

A special thank you goes out to Natalie K. Bard of Cañon City's Local History Center. Natalie could not have been more helpful, professional, or enthusiastic, and her knowledge of the community is both invaluable and enriching. Natalie and Sue Cochran could very well be the best historical researchers in the State of Colorado. Thanks, also, to center director and historian LaDonna L. Gunn for taking on this project, and to Teri Poston and Seth Adams for their priceless contributions.

Gratitude also goes out to the *Cañon City Daily Record* for its ongoing commitment to educate the local community about its frontier heritage, through the work of journalists W. T. "Doc" Little, U. Michael Welch, and John Lemons.

Kathleen McCaslin

To Kathleen McCaslin, my wonderful and always beautiful wife, for her neverending love, support, encouragement and understanding.

To LeAnn McCaslin for her superior editing and astute editorial comments and suggestions – and for her computer wizardry.

LeAnn McCaslin

To the following for their advice, encouragement, or friendship: Louanne Chan, Ivan Millhollin, Pam Munter, Phil Quinn, Linda Neill, Joe and Susan Magri, Tom Feldmann, the Senseney Family, Emily Oldak, Nick Peterson, Jack Blosser, Roye Templeton, Esther Williams, John Rothmann, Noel Neill, Jack Larson, Lou Koza and Stefano Cassolato.

To Linda Steinour for her always tireless and efficient work in putting this book together in a form that can only make a publisher happy.

To Manuel, June, Jackie, Connie, Marcia, Junette, and Darryl.

Finally, to Nick and Tim.

References

American Cowboy. January/February 2003.

Arid America VIII, No. 4. December 1895.

Arkush, R. & Lee, L. *Land Without Ghosts: Chinese Impressions of America from the Mid-Nineteenth Century to the Present.* Berkeley: University of California Press, 1989.

Brown, Sally. *Pioneer Children on the Journey West.* Boulder, Colo: Westview Press, 1995.

Campbell, Rosemae Wells. *From Trappers to Tourists: Fremont County, Colorado, 1830-1950.* Colorado Springs: Century One Press, 1972.

Cañon City Chamber of Commerce. *Cañon City, Colorado: The Gateway to the Rockies.* Cañon City, 1950.

Cañon City Clipper. January 5, 1897; June 29, 1897; July 6, 1897; February 5, 1901; February 8, 1901; August 16, 1901.

Canyon Current. August 1, 2000.

Cañon City Daily Record. March 29, 1906; May 17, 1906; September 20, 1906; February 10, 1910; May 10, 1924; April 16, 1925; December 7, 1929; December 29, 1938; December 18, 1941; January 26, 1956; March 12, 1961; July 20, 1961; April 19, 1967; March 28, 1968; January 9, 1969; November 5, 1969; March 18, 1970; June 4, 1970; December 11, 1970; December 29, 1970; February 12, 1971; August 2, 1971; August 9, 1971; April 4, 1972; June 20, 1972; April 21, 1972; June 29, 1972; July 26, 1972; February 2, 1973; June 27, 1973; September 6, 1973; February 20, 1974; May 6, 1974; June 4, 1974; January 1, 1979; May 23, 1979; June 20, 1979; November 14, 1979; January 5, 1980; May 26, 1980; June 21, 1980; April 18, 1981; July 25, 1981; October 10, 1981; July 10, 1982; January 1, 1983; February 12, 1983; April 30, 1983; December 31, 1983; June 15, 1984; February 23, 1985; May 11, 1985; July 7, 1985; February 28, 1986; March 15, 1986; March 29, 1986; April 12, 1986; December 15, 1986; December 20, 1986; May 6, 1987; April 27, 1988; July 9-10, 1988; February 18-19, 1989; June 17-18, 1989; May 5-6, 1990; December 26, 1990; February 2, 1991; October 21, 1993; January 29, 1996; July 28, 1997; April 30, 1998; September 17, 1998; October 1, 1998; February 4, 1999; February 18, 1999; December 9, 1999; February 10, 2000; February 17, 2000; March 9, 2000; November 23, 2000; June 22, 2001; December 29, 2001.

Cañon City Fruit Day Program. List of Attractions. 1896.

Cañon City Illustrated. Supplement to the Cañon City Daily Record. November 23, 1905.

Cañon City Record. February 5, 1881; December 8, 1888; July 1, 1901; July 25, 1901;
December 19, 1901; March 13, 1902; September 11, 1902; February 21, 1907;
July 18, 1907; March 18, 1909; December 7, 1911; December 7, 1916; September 20, 1917.

Cañon City Record, Building Edition. July 25, 1901.

Cañon City Record, Fruit Day Edition. September 25, 1895.

Cañon City Record, Souvenir Edition. September 30. 1893.

Cañon City Times. October 26, 1905; January 23, 1908; February 9, 1911; July 27, 1911.

Colorado History News. October 1988.

DeCook, Paula & Dexter, S. *Tom Mix: The Cañon City Years - 1910-1911.* Cañon City, 1985.

Denver Post, The. November 2, 1969.

Emrich, David. *Hollywood, Colorado: The Selig Polyscope Company and The Colorado Motion
Picture Company.* Lakewood, CO: Post Modern Company, 1997.

Florence Citizen. January 4, 1996.

Fremont County Farm and Hospital. Records from November 15, 1886 to December 1, 1958.

Fremont County Leader. December 12, 1912; August 21, 1913; May 2, 1914; June 25, 1914;
July 16, 1914; November 18, 1915.

Fremont County Record. August 26, 1882.

Fremont County Extension Homemakers. *Fremont County School Days: From Slate to Apple.*
Canon City: 1986.

Gazette Telegraph. May 19, 1985.

Greenwood Pioneer Cemetery Committee. *Greenwood Cemetery: A Walk Into The Past.*
Cañon City: Barbara Ahart, 2002.

Gunn, LaDonna L. "Establishing an Irrigation-Based Society: Fruit Farming in Cañon City from 1890 to 1910."
Cañon City, Local History Center, April 28, 2003.

Hartman, Emily L. *History Of The Benedictine Sisters Of Chicago.*
Cañon City: St. Scholastica Academy, 1980.

History Of The Arkansas Valley, Colorado. Chicago: O.L. Baskin & Co., 1881.

Little, W.T. "A Century of Service: A History of the Cañon Hotel, 1880-1979." Cañon City, 1979.

Luchetti, Cathy. *Children Of The West: Family Life On The Frontier.*
    New York: W.W. Norton & Co., 2001.

Mathews, A.E. *Canyon City, Colorado, and Its Surroundings.*
    New York: Citizens of Fremont County, 1870.

McGinn, E. & Fisher, C. *If Walls Could Speak.*
    Cañon City: Fremont/Custer Historical Society, 1984.

Mining Gazette. December 10, 1881.

Norris, M.G. "Bud". *The Tom Mix Book.*
    Waynesville, North Carolina: The World Of Tomorrow, 1989.

Osterwald, Doris B. *Rails Thru The Gorge: A Mile By Mile Guide for the Royal Gorge Route.*
    Hugo, Colorado: Western Guideways, Ltd., 2003.

Mazzulla, Fred & Jo. *Al Packer: A Colorado Cannibal.* Denver, 1968.

Mazzulla, Fred & Jo. *Outlaw Albums.* Denver: Hirschfield Press, 1966.

Parker, Dorothy. "The Owl Cigar Store." Fremont/Custer Historical Society, 1988.

Pueblo Chieftan. October 2, 1960; November 13, 1960; August 29, 1971; June 25, 1972;
    June 13, 1976; September 16, 1984; December 4, 1986; June 10, 1989; July 6, 1997;
    November 14, 1999; May 29, 2000; June 9, 2004; July 26, 2004.

Rocky Mountain News. September 21, 1894; February 23, 1916; January 28, 1962;
    March 20, 1965.

Sherwood, Bruce. *All Hail The Tigers: A History Of Cañon City High School - 1880 to 1997.*
    Cañon City: Printing Plus, 1997.

Skyline Ladies Auxiliary #1673. Handmade 1967-1968 Scrapbook honoring World War I veterans.

South Cañon High School Annual. *The Blue and White.* 1912.

Sun, The. September 16, 1954; January 26, 1956.

Technical World. June 1906.

Woodson, Hunter. *Cañon City, Colorado: The Centennial State's Orchard Home.*
    New York: Carson Harper Co., 1899.

Local History Center, Cañon City

Observation Point - Royal Gorge, C. 1910.